Praise for **Frugal Indulgents**

"If only *Frugal Indulgents* had been written years ago, with the money I'd have saved on therapy, drugs, moving apartments five times a year, and recovering from bad relationships, I might have actually been able to do something useful with my life."
—Elizabeth Wurtzel, author of *Prozac Nation*

"*Frugal Indulgents* is a survival guide of the best sort: if Bolonik and Griffin's practical advice doesn't rescue you from the sorrows of penury, their deadpan irony and sure-fire wit will grant you the distance you need to laugh at your predicament."
—Douglas Rushkoff, author of
Playing the Future and *Media Virus*

"Kera Bolonik and Jennifer Griffin are the savv slinkstresses of frugal city swank. A veritable extravaganza of snazzy quizlettes, enthralling profiles, and smart nibblies about how to cultivate affordable *bouviessence*.* This book made me want to hang with the hero[ine]s who swing on a shoestring."
—Francesca Lia Block, author of
Girl Goddess #9 and *Weetzie Bat*

**bouviessence:* in honor of the queen of grace, Jacqueline Bouvier Kennedy Onassis, this word signifies glamour at all times for all occasions

Frugal Indulgents

HOW TO CULTIVATE DECADENCE
WHEN YOUR AGE AND SALARY ARE
UNDER 30

Kera Bolonik and Jennifer Griffin

An Owl Book

HENRY HOLT AND COMPANY · NEW YORK

Henry Holt and Company, Inc.
Publishers since 1866
115 West 18th Street
New York, NY 10011

Henry Holt® is a registered trademark of
Henry Holt and Company, Inc.

Library of Congress Cataloging-in-Publication Data
Bolonik, Kera.
Frugal indulgents: how to cultivate decadence when your age and
salary are under 30 / by Kera Bolonik and Jennifer Griffin.
p.   cm.
"An owl book."
1. Consumer education—United States.   2. Generation X—United
States—Life skills guides.   3. Young adults—United States—Life
skills guides.   4. Saving and thrift—United States.   5. Life style—
United States.   I. Griffin, Jennifer.   II. Title.
TX336.B65   1997   96-45270
640'.73'0973—dc21   CIP

ISBN 0-8050-4718-2

Henry Holt books are available for special promotions
and premiums. For details contact: Director, Special Markets.

First Edition—1997

Designed by Betty Lew

Printed in the United States of America
All first editions are printed on acid-free paper.∞

1   3   5   7   9   10   8   6   4   2

To the memory of
Lisa "Oni" Monteleone,
a Frugal Indulgent pioneer, dear friend,
and an early advocate of this book.

And to Justin Powell,
resourceful and generous—
a whirlwind of inspiration.

CONTENTS

ACKNOWLEDGMENTS

Special thanks to Larry Ashmead, Sharon Bowers, Funda Duyal, Evan Gaffney, Moina Noor, Suzanne Oaks, Andrea Schneeman, Lilian Shia, Darcy Tromanhauser, Jennifer Unter, Lydia Wills, and Elizabeth Wurtzel.

Hearty thanks to Kerry Acker, Jason Bagdade, Todd Beeton, Lisa Berkowitz, the Boloniks, Wesley Brown, Ashok Chaudhari, Anne Cole, Pattie Cronin, Claudia Cross, Dan Cuddy, Airié Dekidjiev, Meaghan Dowling, Janice Easton, Barbara Eaton, Mimi Engel, Carl Ferrero, Lauren Fischer, Julia and Stephen Francis, Diane Frieden, Susan Friedland, Todd Goodale, Amanda Gordon, Mary Gossy, Evie Greenbaum, the Griffins, Jill Grinberg, Kathleen Hackett, David Hawk, Laura Impert, Martha Jessup, Penny Kaganoff, John Kahrs, Ariel Kaminer, Terry Karten, Vikash Lall, Clio Manuelian, Paul Marcarelli, Lisa Mayne, Jerry Orabona, Alicia Ostriker, Tim Parrish, Aisha Piracha, David Rakoff, Robin Raisfeld, Scott Renschler, Lisa Ryers, Jennie Scharf, Sarah Scheffel, Christopher Schelling, Arthur Schwartz, Miranda Schwartz, Phyllis Silverstein, Pamela Talese, Sebastian Trainor, Angelina Cusano Wallent, and Joshua Wilkes for their stories, words of vocabulary, and support.

"THAT MAN IS RICHEST WHOSE PLEASURES ARE THE CHEAPEST."

—HENRY DAVID THOREAU

Introduction

The Frugal Indulgent Manifesto

"MONEY CAN DO HORRIBLE THINGS TO IGNORANT PEOPLE."
                                           —DIANA VREELAND

When we set out to write this guide, we considered those who most inspired us in our inexpensive pursuit of urban happiness. We analyzed and learned to emulate our role models: Fran Lebowitz, expert in urban wit, cocktail banter, and country home crashing; David Niven, the gentleman Hugh Grant turned out not to be; Sonic Youth's Kim Gordon, socially graceful, artistic provocateuse; Jacqueline Bouvier Kennedy Onassis, who never let her glamour guard down; Quentin Crisp, insolvent but exalted; and Diana Vreeland, arbiter of fashion, and fashioner of arbitrary aphorisms—to name just a few. From these people and our own clever friends we have learned not only how to survive, but how to do so with style, wit, and grace.

After living in a large city for a few years, we understand a thing or two about urbanity and how to cultivate it. We have no trust funds, no sugar daddies, no family-based financial support, and neither of us has a job that pays more than a *minimal* wage. While our funds are spotty, our intuition is constant, and yours can be too. We'll show you whom to watch, and what to co-opt from them.

Frugal Indulgents discusses the appropriate means of appropriating ways of living; having great intercourse, conversational and otherwise; buying *hot* couture; differentiating between friends and faux; strengthening your dollar (and we do mean dollar!); and entertaining yourself and others with finesse. Most of all, *Frugal Indulgents* celebrates liberation from capital: True *bouviessence* (glamour at all times for all occasions) is, believe it or not, independent of money.

This book is written for aspiring urbanites who are young and hip, smart and liberally educated, provocative, tasteful, and savvy, as well as bereft of the financial resources to create the kind of lifestyles to which they should be accustomed.

We are a generation who, despite media misdepiction, are serious about our careers, serious about our play, serious about our self-representation. We were raised on the misconception that style and money are codependent. We know better now. Cleverness and savvy are the better parts of elegance, and they are at the fingertips of the curious reader. We will show you how our friends have scored lovely low-rent apartments; dressed themselves in the finest threads on a shoestring budget; entertained themselves for hours on ten dollars or less; found ways to appease their screaming libidos with boys and girls alike (sex is free, after all); and fled town for country without having to save pennies all year.

We will teach you how to use *expenseploitation*—the art of milking an expense account, be it yours or a friend's—to feed yourself to the gills; culture your pearls of wisdom for cocktail banter; host non-potluck dinner parties without overspending; take in decadent urban scenery by making one martini last a good long time. Most important, we will help you decide when to be frugal and when to indulge. After reading *Frugal Indulgents,* picking up a few anecdotal tricks of the trade and emulating styles that work, you will feel that you are finally *living,* not just surviving.

There are certain basic principles that apply to every aspect of life as a Frugal Indulgent. These concern behavior and attitude. Before we begin, we feel it is important that you know where we're coming from, so we've penned the Frugal Indulgent Manifesto for your reading pleasure. Follow these rules, and relish your imminently grand lifestyle.

1. **Never Act Your Age or Your Income.** You may be young and poor, but you are also smart and tasteful. Try to let the latter qualities overshadow the former.

2. **Aim High.** If you assume you can't fly first class on your budget, you never will. Assume that you deserve the best, and try to get it. Sometimes you'll prevail.

3. **Exude Confidence.** The surer you appear to be about yourself, the surer others will be about you. If you act like you own the place, more often than not you will be treated like the owner.

4. **Fake It.** If you are not confident, you can fake it. You think you aren't fitting in at an event? Think you're not qualified for a job? Not worthy of a date with a fabulous person? Shut up about it and pretend that you are. Chances are you are the only one who knows your shortcomings. If you act the part, you may get away with it.

5. **Never Apologize.** The soufflé has fallen. You ate the salad with the entree fork. Your sofa has seen better days: So what? Apologies put people on edge. Aplomb in the face of adversity puts them at ease. Friends and strangers will admire you for having the silent courage to showcase your quirks. Smile and keep dancing.

6. **Be Curious.** Read everything. Talk to everyone. Ask questions. The more inquisitive you are, the more information you'll gather. As the "Schoolhouse Rock" people used to say, knowledge is power.

A FEW BONS MOTS

Cunning Lingo

ACTION FIGURE Those who do not travel light. For example, Gordon considers himself a model/actor/carpenter/lawyer. If we were to market a "Gordon" doll, he would come equipped with head shot, portfolio, hammer, and laptop in hand.

A IDIOT Pronounced "uh idiot." The term for this type of person is grammatically incorrect to stress the dumbocity of the subject. On the continuum of stupidity, this person would probably be found a notch above retarded, a notch below a rube.

BOUVIESSENCE In honor of the queen of grace, this word signifies glamour at all times for all occasions. You run out to get the paper, but not before donning a scarf, sunglasses, lipstick, and mules. So what if you haven't showered?

CAUSEMOPOLITAN Of or relating to socialites whose politics are determined by who's throwing the most fabulous benefit, auction, etc. For example: "Causemopolitan Linda was never really interested in ecological issues until she heard about that great Sotheby's cocktail party hosted by Al Gore."

DECADENCIA Decadencia is to decadence what intelligentsia is to intellects. The decadencia are in the know about splurging, frugal-indulgently speaking.

DISS-ARRAY When all the couples in your social circle break up en masse. They've *dissed* one another, and now there is an *array* of lovers to choose from.

DUMPSTER The opposite of a hipster. A person who wears ugly clothing without the irony that would elevate them to hip.

DWI Drinking while intoxicated. Beyond blotto.

EXFRIENDABLE An expendable friend. If you find you are doing all the work in a relationship, that your generosity comes without reciprocation, and this friend is of no use to you, he or she is exfriendable.

EXPENSEPLOITATION The act of treating yourself and a friend working in a field marginally related to yours to lunch on the company card.

FAUX REAL So fake they're cool; also, so passé they're retro. "Are those pearls *faux real?*"

FYI Frugalize Your Indulgence. You may indulge, but if you can get it on sale, get it from someone as a gift, or get it for free, please do so.

GLAMBIDEXTROUS The ability to look fabulous with the poise to make it seem easy.

GLAMBIVALENT Do I look good or not? It's so hard to say.

GLAMOUREXIA NERVOSA An anxietal disorder, not unlike agoraphobia, in which one misses social engagements due to one or more of the following problems: a bad hair day, a fashion crisis, a lack of clean laundry, acne and/or blemishes, etc. There is a certain degree of self-importance operating here: The sufferer feels that by going out, s/he can uglify the world by merely making an appearance.

HEINOIS (rhymes with "c'est moi"). Beyond heinous. This superlative is so strong that English cannot convey the sentiment. Besides, it sounds better with a French twist. What doesn't?

INFAUXMATION A means to live in the know without the bother of learning firsthand. Gathering infauxmation is the ultimate act of appropriation, just short of becoming a poseur. You haven't read the book, seen the film, or eaten at the restaurant, but you've read the reviews, synthesized the information, and formulated a definitive opinion on the subject.

LICENSE TO SLACK A euphemism for trust fund.

LIFE-DEFERRAL PLAN (LDP) The act of putting "real" life off for an indefinite period of time: graduate school, going abroad, driving cross-country, etc. College loans are deferred, parents still support you, and credit card dependence is more acceptable than ever.

LOSERATI Remember those kids in high school who made your life a living hell? Well, they still live at Mom and Dad's in the 'burbs with no plans to move, get a real job, or find new friends. They hang out at the local pub every night, oblivious to the city just a few short miles away, and they've gotten flabby and dull. They comprise the loserati.

MAUDE (adj.) Describes how some people look in vintage clothing. *Maude* is the opposite of *mod*. That is to say, they look more like *Maude*'s Bea Arthur than *The Avengers*' Diana Rigg. Not a good thing.

NOUVEAU PAUVRE A class of people who have the tastes and expectations of the bourgeoisie without the financial trappings. Frugal Indulgents are of this class.

P.O.W. Piece of Work. Someone who exceeds the call of idiocy.

QUASIMODE A breath away from fashionable. You're very close, but not quite at the finish line. For example, great suit but bad shoe choice. A quasimode is not as bad as a *dumpster*.

QUASMOPOLITAN One who plays and/or works in the big city, but lives in its outskirts. In Chicago these would-be urbanites are referred to as "708s," for their area code.

SALVATION ARMANI Maximizing your indulgence, even if it means risking shaking a tin cup in front of Neiman Marcus. "Because Carl had a moment of Salvation Armani when he bought that Paul Smith four-button, single-breasted linen suit against his better budget, he will be spending the summer couch-hopping (but doing so in style)."

SAVV Indulgent cunning. Derived from *savvy*.

SID VICIOUS CIRCLE A literary salon comprising self-proclaimed cutting-edge sorts masquerading as writers who've yet to cough up their opuses.

SIMULACRA-WEAR Clothing that is a copy for which there is no original. Think Gap pocket T-shirt.

SKRÜ SORBET The post–breakup one-night stand. It acts as a cleansing of the genital palate, whereby the *jilted* can relish the fact that the last person s/he bedded was not the *jilter.*

SLUTERRIFIC A really good one-night stand.

SLUTROCITY A really bad one-night stand.

VREELANDISH A daring move that would be outlandish if you weren't pulling it off so well. Recall the boldness of the namesake, grande dame of red walls, pink bulletin boards, and outrageous leopard-print upholstery. "Your mango LaCroix bodysuit is positively Vreelandish, Edina."

Your Fabulous Apartment
Be It Never So Humble

"COME MOVE IN A NEW DIMENSION."
—PATTI SMITH, "AIN'T IT STRANGE"

Depending on where you decide to live, finding an apartment may be more difficult than landing a job in the midst of a recession. Before you venture through the apartment listings in your local newspaper, laundromat, or on-line bulletin board, it is important to know what you're willing to spend, and what you're willing to settle for. For some, housing acceptability hinges on accessibility. For others, it hinges on affordability. In this chapter, as in the following chapter, we will help you decide which you find more important: a fabulous spread with a few good threads, or a full wardrobe with an apartment only you will see (assuming you can't have both). Part of being a Frugal Indulgent entails embracing compromise, which humbles your bourgeois soul.

In this chapter, we will deconstruct the semiotics of housing advertisements; recount amazing tales of rental heroism, good fortune, and disaster; and let you in on the key to finding the apartment of your dreams: Deal with a real estate broker only as a last resort.

In nowhere but the real estate scramble is it more evident that milking every resource available to you is the way to find the best deal. This means broadcasting your plight to everyone you know.

Find out who is tired of the city and moving to the 'burbs or back-woods; which couples have decided to move in together, or split apart. Befriend academic types who may have to surrender their places to go to Mongolia on a fellowship or to teach literature in the Southernmost University of Tennessee. You might not get a great deal on the first go-round, so always keep your eyes open for a better offer. Eating takeout in the kitchenette/bathroom of your three-month sublet is just a snack in a waiting room. Look out the window. You may think you're facing a brick wall, but it's really opportunity meeting your gaze. Once you get a sense of the neighborhood and make some contacts, you will soon be moving into the apartment of your choice. Besides, when you start out small, you can only improve, so call the Chinese restaurant across the street for some egg rolls, and keep scanning the ads for places with a fully operating eat-in kitchen.

Once you've found your space, you've got to fill it. A house is not a home without fun furnishings. Whether you decide to buy, borrow, or steal (from your family), there are strategies here for you that will ensure you are surrounded by all the pots, pans, chairs, and other tchotchkes and furniture you can pack into your new nest.

THE APARTMENT QUIZ

1   David's New York City apartment building has just gone co-op and he's been invited to buy the place (a hundred and fifty grand for a three-hundred-square-foot studio) or get out. Obviously,

it's time for David to go apartment hunting. Some creative living arrangements present themselves. Which is the one for him?

a. A Gramercy Park (equidistant to both midtown and the East Village) rental in a gigantic loft. He would be one of three full-time illegal subletters. The owner of the co-op apartment, a Jungian analyst, has an office there and sleeps over in the spare bedroom two nights a week. The rent is six hundred dollars for a gigantic room of his own with French doors and a beautifully furnished living room.

b. An apartment on Roosevelt Island, the small Manhattan suburb accessible by subway, tram, and car (the only road goes via distant Queens). David's unit, like all the others in the two apartment complexes on the island, would be new and bright, safe and characterless. The rent is six hundred dollars.

c. A tiny Manhattan studio on the quiet, safe, and deadly dull Upper East Side. There he'd have a kitchenette in his room and a shower stall next to the oven, with a special little toilet closet (the only closet in the entire apartment). But it would be a place all his own, not to mention its proximity to all trains, and the price: six hundred dollars.

d. A three-bedroom, two–full bath in flavorless midtown Manhattan with three other friends. One of the three roommates shares the master bedroom with roommate number two, who is only home in the evenings, as he sleeps at his lover's apartment every night. Pluses: David would have his own room, space to entertain, light, security, utilities split four ways, easy commute to work. Minuses: Noisy as hell, strange neighborhood, reduced privacy, too much junk mail, occasional lost phone messages.

2 Kate and Chloe have been involved for three months. Each of their leases is up in six weeks. It seems a waste of money to have two apartments in the Brookline section of Boston, especially

since the women spend so much time together. The honeymoon is far from over, and could probably endure a yearlong lease. Besides, it takes two to find one fabulous apartment. They should throw caution to the wind and get a place together. True or False?

3. Isabel and Ron have been involved on and off for three years. He has impeccable taste—a beautiful ottoman, a complete set of Harlequinware (inherited from Mom)—and meticulous manners. Isabel is a fabulous cook, and has a TV, VCR, and an antique wrought-iron queen-size bed. Ron is a consultant at a major architectural firm. Isabel is an assistant professor of art history at DePaul University in Chicago. The two could have a gorgeous setup if they agreed that their relationship could weather living together. Isabel will move in with Ron with hopes for marriage. Ron is psyched to split the rent and utilities, and thinks living together could be a blast. They should shack up. True or False?

4. Mom and Dad live on Bainbridge Island, just a ferry ride away from downtown Seattle, where Susan has just been hired to work full-time at a bookstore. The rents in Capitol Hill are high, and the 'rents on Bainbridge Island don't seem as irritating as they did in high school. They've offered to house Susan for free and give her the 1985 Volvo she's been coveting since its purchase. (Dad is getting a new car.) Can she survive living with her parents?

5. ESSAY QUESTION: You've just arrived in San Francisco with a job in your pocket and a home on your old college roommate's couch. While you don't want to overstay your welcome, you also don't want to settle into any old apartment. Because Jane is your only friend in the San Francisco area, the dependence factor is high. She tells you of two housing possibilities: The first, a rent-controlled studio on Castro Street with beautiful moldings, hardwood floors, a working fireplace, high ceilings, an eat-in kitchen,

and a washer and dryer. The second, a share in a four-bedroom apartment with three preexisting roommates in a co-op style environment, also on Castro. The latter is available in three weeks, and though it is a nice apartment, you aren't sure that you are ready for such a big, new family. The former sounds perfect, and is presently occupied by Jane's colleague Andrea. After eight months of glee, Andrea has decided that she and Greg are ready to live together. She can move out in six weeks at the earliest. You want to get out of Jane's hair, but part of you wants to hold out for the beautiful apartment that can, allegedly, be yours in time. The discrepancy is two hundred dollars in favor of the share. What to do?

ANSWERS

1. **C** or **d**, depending on whether David is roommate-compatible. Some people's tolerance for roommates expires soon after they move out of that off-campus rattrap they shared with five friends during their senior year of college. These types select **c**. If David does like roommates, he can enjoy discounted utility bills and more space for entertaining if he selects **d**. **B** is his next best bet. There's something to be said for spaciousness, especially in Manhattan. But David is not going to be able to dine out or catch a movie on the spur of the moment from this distant location. And what will he use for bait to lure friends to his parties? **A** is a bad move. Who wants to spend any extra time with a Jungian, not to mention three extra strangers? He will have no privacy, and he might as well move in with his parents.

2. **True.** So far, so good. If there are no glaring problems after your ninety-day warranty is up, the chance to play house and save money may make it worth taking the plunge. Can they get a month-to-month lease? They should look into it. Caution: A year

in claustrophobic relationship hell lasts a lot longer than say, a year in Provence.

3. **False.** It's tempting given the complementary talents and possessions, but they're not enough to sustain the wear and tear of an everyday relationship. Never move in with someone who has commitment problems. And Isabel shouldn't kid herself by thinking he'll marry her. His reasons for shacking up are financial and in his favor; hers include a long-term vision to which he is blind.

4. **No.** Never ever ever. Don't be tempted by the car; it is a false promise of sovereignty. The pluses: full fridge, free rent. Minuses: no privacy, no sex, no drugs, nervous breakdown. Not worth it.

5. Unless you are making absolutely no money, take that gorgeous studio. But how secure is that relationship between Andrea and her boyfriend? Assuming that their love lasts for the duration of the sublet, will you be able to take over the lease? These are concerns you should heed while responding to the question. On the upside, Andrea is a friend of Jane's, and Jane is a friend of yours, so **a** = **c**, and Andrea may let you start moving in some of your belongings early. A share is not *so* bad, especially if you've just graduated from college; your standards are already sub. Besides, the roommates are generous, nice, and cool. There is money to be saved and an instant social life to be gained. You can't go wrong with either of these options, so do take one of them.

METROPOLIS NOW: ON YOUR OWN IN THE BIG CITY

"FIND A CITY, FIND MYSELF A CITY TO LIVE IN."
—THE TALKING HEADS, "CITIES"

You've had it. You've held every job your college and hometowns have had to offer. You've dated everyone you've ever known. Every bridge has been burnt, rebuilt, and burnt again, and all before you've begun your adult life. It is time to being anew, to reconstruct your identity, to brave the new world. You've decided to move to a big city. We applaud you.

Now you are faced with some daunting tasks. You have to hunt and gather an apartment, a job, some friends. People often move to a city in which they have one but not all of these. Never fear. You are a Frugal Indulgent, if not now, then soon. It's time to start stalking your prey, on bulletin boards on-line and off. As you begin to sort out where you want to live, we suggest the following:

- *Gather newspapers from the intended city.* This enables you to get a sense of the urban culture, as well as gauge rental climates and job prospects.
- *Hunt down friends who can house your body all night long.* It is much easier to move to a city where you know and can tolerate at least one person. It affords you a couch to stay on while looking for your new home. That person becomes an ambassador of sorts, giving you housing leads, introducing you to some of his crowd, and informing you of job openings and contacts. (Your sponsoring friend has as strong an interest in your apartment search as you do: he wants you off of his futon and onto your own.) If you are moving to Dallas from rural Wisconsin, it is time to dust off your old school phone directories and ask if your fellow alumni have older hipster sibs willing to take you under their veteran wings. The

squeaky wheel gets the contacts, so get on the horn and honk loudly.

- *Job hunt.* You may find that landing a job is easier than landing an apartment, even during a recession. A job enables you to meet people who may lead you to social and housing windfalls. You can query your newfound pals about which parts of the neighborhood are happening and which rents are out of the question. You may even pick up some potential roommates along the way.

- *Gather some housemates, or hunt for a studio.* You may find that after years of living with four or ten roommates in a house in Athens, Georgia, the idea has worn out its welcome, and a studio of your own is all you ask. However, you may find that living with roommates eases your postcollegiate transition into the land of the lost. Or, you may be fortunate enough to have a lover, and even more fortunate to get him or her to move to the city with you.

- *Gather your resources wherever they lie.* If you have any institutional connections, however tenuous, use them to find housing. Hospitals, universities, and very large corporations are particularly fertile hunting grounds.

Whatever your situation, you've made an important, and commendable, decision. You want your metropolis, and you want it now. Hey, Courtney Love wants "to be the girl with the most cake"; why shouldn't you? Pack up the U-Haul and get out of suburbia.

REALTY BITES: FINDING AN APARTMENT

"WHAT FRESH HELL IS THIS?"

—DOROTHY PARKER

You have found a city to live in, but you are starting to overstay your welcome on the couch of your friends, acquaintances, relatives. Whether you have settled your employment issues or not, you must embark on the hell that awaits you: figuring out where to live and how to finance it. Possibilities to contemplate:

Taking a lover A big one-bedroom that is unaffordable on one income becomes comfortable for two.

Taking a roommate, or two Are you a roommate type or a lone wolf? While having too many roommates may prove to be a never-ending house of din, having one or two may prove to be quite beneficial. You double, even triple, your wardrobe. The bills are split, two, three, four ways. People take messages for you when you're out, split household chores . . . the benefits are endless. Besides, living alone may drive some to high phone bills, excessive drinking binges, and agoraphobia, all developed out of sheer loneliness. When you assess your housing values you must be honest with yourself, especially before signing your life away for a year at a time on the dotted line.

Taking a place all to yourself The only noise you create is your own. While it tends to be pricey, there is no one to argue with but yourself. You can prance around your own place in your birthday suit, bring home anyone you want without worrying about causing an immediate scandal, and decorate to your taste. The key benefit to living alone: privacy. It's all yours when you pay for it. And because you don't need to consult with anyone else, apartment hunting proves easier. It may not be the ideal option if you just moved to a new city, as it makes it very easy to feel isolated, but if you have established your presence in your city circuit, you may want your own sacred sanctuary.

Once a decision is made, you are ready to explore the possibilities, as well as the impossibilities. Tackle the apartment listings in the local papers, but not before consulting with the locals about realistic expectations. Have work chums, friends of friends, and the like take you around several neighborhoods to give you a sense of what to look for. If you are not entirely sure that this is the city or the living situation for you, try to find a sublet for a few months. This way, you provide yourself with the opportunity to city hop, get a better sense of city accommodations in relation to your needs, and begin to acclimate to the metropolis.

Renting a room in a house, finding a communal co-op situation, or joining a roommate-filled apartment on a month-to-month lease are other means of testing the waters. Whatever you do, use every resource available to you: on-line listings, Laundromat and food co-op bulletin boards, word-of-mouth leads, local papers. You just may land a rent-controlled palace, securing you a comfortable living situation for years to come. Finding the home that suits you may take some jockeying around, but remember, Rome wasn't built in a day, so don't expect that your nest will be either.

Profile

NOT TOO CLOSE FOR COMFORT

ELLEN AND FRANK

Ellen has been living in New York for four years, most of that time in Brooklyn. While jockeying her career about, she lost track of time and saw her lease run out, with no plans for her next move. Old pal Frank to the rescue. Frank lives in a small studio apartment up near Columbia University in Manhattan, where he is the proud owner of a trundle bed with Ellen's name written all over it. Needless to say, until then, their friendship had never been tested in such an intimate manner. Ellen moved in, paid half of the already cheap rent, and tried to be as gracious a guest as anyone sharing a small apartment could. Since her attempts at not imposing were strong, Frank returned the favor by not imposing a time limit, providing Ellen with just enough time to find a good living arrangement. During this course of events, Ellen and Frank happened upon the secret to a long-lasting marriage: separate beds, no sex, and as much space as two people with publishing jobs and a studio can provide. Two months later, Ellen's brother scored a full-time job in town, and got a large two-bedroom in lower Manhattan. Tearfully yet cheerfully, Ellen moved into a spacious room with her beloved sib.

John and Christine

Even more like a marriage, here's the story of a gay man and a straight woman in an ideal situation. Boasting ten years of friendship, John and Christine decided to move into Manhattan together from their respective apartments in Brooklyn. The pickings were slim, so they settled for a *conv. 2-bdrm* (really a *conv. 1-bdrm*). Christine, however, was the sole owner of a bed, as John was holding out for the wrought-iron bed he'd ordered. Being the generous friend that she is, Christine shared her bed with cot-less John during the six to eight-week wait, and the two grew so comfy sleeping platonically together that John canceled his order. One year later, the two continue to share a bed in bliss, though they each take a time-out when they bed another, at the lover-of-the-moment's apartment.

Profile

The Ancestral Home

Miranda

When people first visit Miranda's upper Upper West Side Manhattan apartment, they behave as though they were on a tour of Windsor Castle, with disbelieving *oohs* and *ahs,* and the desire to inquire about her finances. Her apartment is as disparate in scope from those of her friends as Princess Diana's first London flat must have been from the British landmark. And Miranda's apartment is as much her birthright as Windsor is the Royal Family's. It is her ancestral home.

The apartment has three spacious bedrooms, a long hallway, a bath and a half, an eat-in kitchen with a pantry, ample closet space, a living room, and a dining room. The floors are hardwood parquet; the ceilings high; the walls adorned with moldings; the windows large, plentiful, and facing the cheerful greenery of Riverside Park. The rent is $585 a month. Miranda has a roommate, so each pays a meager $292.50.

How can this be? Miranda's parents moved into the rent-controlled apartment before she was born in 1968. They raised Miranda and her sister there, and when they upgraded apartments in 1982, they decided to hang on to this one. The apartment has always been occupied—by Miranda, by her sister, and by their friends. The inhabitants come and go with the freedom that palatial space and tiny expense afford. In this world nothing is certain but death, taxes, and that Miranda is never moving out of her apartment.

The Semiotics of Housing Listings

Unpack your collection of Roland Barthes. It's time for a semiotics lesson. Sorting through the signs of the *Times,* the *Tribune*s, the *Herald*s, can be rather confusing. If you've just moved to a new city, and are not familiar with your surroundings, the language of the classified ads can be misleading. Once you've assessed your housing budget, you need to find out what your money can really buy. Here is a list of the most frequently used terms in housing advertisements, and what they really mean:

BALCONY Fire escape.

CONTINENTAL Tub in the kitchen, one sink in the whole spread, toilet closet off the kitchen. No hallway, just a multipurpose alcove used for bathing and cooking. Bedrooms off either side usually in L formation. Common in NYC.

CONV 1-BDRM Literally means "convertible one-bedroom." In real life, it is a studio.

COZY Also appears as "quaint" and "charming." Really means "minuscule." Everything is within reach from bed:

You can turn on the sink and greet visitors without getting out of bed.

DRMN Doorman. Utterly unaffordable.

DUPLEX A loft bed with a ladder. If it is a real duplex—a two-story apartment—it is more than likely to be out of your price range, even with roommates.

EIK Eat-in kitchen, meaning you can pull a chair up to the kitchen counter for self-dining.

ELEV Elevator, not necessarily operating or affordable.

EXPO BRK Exposed brick. No wall hangings for you. Though some brick walls are charming in the true sense of the word, beware of the apartment that resembles the basement of a comedy club.

FLEX 2 A possible two-bedroom apartment. Like the *conv. 1-bdrm,* more likely to be a one-bedroom with a walk-in closet.

HEALTH CLUB Either too expensive, or equipped with a manual Stairmaster (seven-floor walkup).

LRG Large. See *cozy.*

MINI-LOFT Studio apartment.

NR ALL TRNSPTN Near all transportation. The building is located atop a subway station.

NR WATER Near water. Flooding or leaking potential if they're being honest. Also, near is a relative term. Is the water within sight of your building? Is it a body of water you'd want to be near? In Chicago, for example, is it near scenic Lake Michigan, or the sludgy Chicago River?

NO FEE Meaning, you don't need to pay a realtor a finder's fee (often 10 percent of the year's rent). Bonus!

1 MONTH FREE RENT Totally implausible. Lies, lies, lies.

PENTHOUSE Attic studio. À la *La Bohème*.

PREWAR Which war? Revolutionary? Civil? It may look like the apartment got shelled. Moldings may be falling apart. Yellow water and fickle heat guaranteed.

RAILROAD No hallway means no privacy. You have to traipse through your roommate's bedroom to get to the bathroom.

RENO Newly renovated. Often signifies a fresh paint job, wiped down linoleum floors in the eik, and walls you can blow over with a straw.

RENT STBLZ Rent stabilized. A rarity. You've scored big and long-term if you've found one of these.

SPAC Spacious. See *cozy*.

UTIL INCL Utilities included in your rent. In other words, you can have the heat on all summer, free of cost.

WBF Wood-burning fireplace. Does not apply to our readership. You may have seen one of these on your high school trip to Vermont. Savor the memory.

W/VU With view ... of the brick building next door and, if you're lucky, kinky neighbors.

THE HOUSE OF DEARTH: FURNISHING YOUR ABODE

"HAVE NOTHING IN YOUR HOME THAT YOU DO NOT KNOW TO BE USE-
FUL OR BELIEVE TO BE BEAUTIFUL."

—WILLIAM MORRIS

You've settled into a city, found yourself a home. Next stop: furniture! You need a place for your weary head, your wearying takeout, your clothes, books. There are several ways to go about this, and you'll be surprised to find what an inexpensive pursuit of happiness it is.

Here are the things you need to buy right off: a bed, bookcase(s), a kitchen table. Sure, you can hold out for hand-me-downs, but who wants to sleep on the hard floor for weeks at a time? Stacking books, files, and CDs on the floor gets a bit messy, and eating off the floor should be reserved for pets and Dustbusters. These are worthy investments.

Once the minimalism wears thin, you may want to start filling your home with a few other items. There are those things you buy for pennies, and there are those you acquire from the curbside selection. Big money should not be spent on the following:

Chairs Unless you have money to burn, never buy a chair. There is always an orphaned chair looking for a new home.

Couches These plush items are often objets de curbside salvation or inheritance.

Desks, bureaus These can be picked up for pennies at the Salvation Army or stoop/garage/yard sales.

Plates and silverware Often inherited from family members, or accumulated from former roommates. While acquiring eating utensils may take some time, be patient. You'll kick yourself for having dropped two hundred dollars at Crate & Barrel on a complete set of kitchenware when your mom's friend decides to put her pantry through a makeover and gives you a brilliant set of Fiestaware.

Patience is not only a virtue, it is a key to metropolitan life. Often your material wishes for housewares will come through. While you are waiting for fate to intervene and drop a set of silver into your lap, collect plasticware from the local takeout restaurant. A few orders of hot-and-sour soup and curried chicken later, you'll have service for four.

There are things one can buy at stores like Ikea, Ames, Caldor, and the like. Bookcases are always safe. They are usually inexpensive, and it rarely matters what they look like, since you will be filling them up in no time. If you find that free kitchen tables and desks are hard to come by, it is also okay to buy new. Do not buy bureaus or wardrobe closets at one of these stores—now you are starting to push your Ikea luck. And never buy a couch at a cheap store, not merely because it is an unnecessary expense, but because cheaply made couches are at once uncomfortable, and of poor and characterless quality. (See Profile: Lisa, Lisa, and the Couch Jam, page 30).

As you will note in forthcoming chapters, namely "Entertainment," befriending the older, wiser, and cash-endowed is filled with benefits. In the case of furnishings, some of your slightly older friends may want to upgrade from their own curbside selections, and buy a proper bed, a dining room table, new bookcases, a set of bureau drawers, a top-notch air conditioner. These friends and/or family members wouldn't want to waste their golden oldies by merely tossing them in the garbage. If they call to ask you if you need a Hoover vacuum cleaner or an old marble coffee table, take it!

Save your money for rent, dinners, drinks, parties, and clothes. Good furniture is something no money can buy, so don't.

Furnished upon Request

Mimi

After living at her parents' home in the 'burbs for a year after college, Mimi's tolerance level for her folks, and theirs for her, was dropping rapidly. Mimi took a deep breath, and checked her Filofax for old and new friends wanting to move into Chicago. Once she found two friends to live with, she rummaged through the *Chicago Reader* to find an apartment to house three women. They scored a place. On to phase two: furnishings. Mimi is not one to spend money on furniture, and why should she? Her mother was so thrilled that her daughter was moving to the city and out of her house, that soon the word was out to all that Mimi needed some groovy furnishings. It wasn't too long ago that Mimi's mom had replaced her Aztec-motif leather-and-wood chairs. Gayle, Mom's friend, had begun a business hand-painting wooden furniture, and donated a few hours of her services. And after Cathy's second divorce it was time to do a little spring cleaning. To Mimi's delight, her apartment was soon filled with historical objets d'art. (Mom's chairs sure brought back memories of couples hanging out with glasses of wine just before embarking on an evening of disco fever at Zorine's à la *Saturday Night Fever.*) The kitsch factor runs high, butts have homes, and the apartment looks fabulous. Not a dime spent.

Lisa, Lisa, and the Couch Jam

Todd, Lisa, and Lisa made a terrible mistake. Back in 1990 the three went to Ikea to buy a blue Elsa couch with a foldout bed to offer to slumbering guests. Within two weeks, a slab of wood started to jut out like a bone in a compound fracture, and the piece of furniture came to be known simply as "The Uncomfortable Couch." Offered only to those guests the hosts didn't want to stay too long, The Uncomfortable Couch squatted in the residence for several years, becoming at once the bane of the housemates' existence, and the butt of many a joke. When the three roommates finally dragged the couch to the street corner to be picked up by the sanitation department, *a idiot* spotted it, returned with several friends and his Impala, and drove off with the odious thing.

Not only did the couch provide years of discomfort, embarrassment, and remorse for wasted money spent, but it couldn't even provide joy for its next owner, unbeknownst to him.

Susannah

Susannah is a chair addict; whenever she finds a stray on the street, she cannot resist dragging it home to strip and repaint. On her way to dinner with her roommates one night, she spotted a grimy patio bench peeking out of a sidewalk trash heap. Its frame was a dirty, white wrought iron; it's lima bean–shaped padded-Naugahyde seat was covered with greasy black soot. Susannah saw through the slime, and her heart leapt for joy. She tried to convince her roommates to carry the one-of-a-kind piece back to the apartment, but, just blocks from the restaurant, they wouldn't have it. To placate her whining, they agreed that if the bench were still unclaimed on their way home from dinner, they would help her then.

When they returned to the site, there was much rejoicing: The bench was waiting for them. They dislodged it from the trash heap and lugged it home, where Susannah rubbed the seat with baking soda, vinegar, and hot water and scraped the coating off with an old library card. Voila! The seat was white, intact, and a fit companion for the rest of the roommates' funky furniture.

Moral: He who hesitates is usually lost. Susannah got lucky on this one.

Kathleen

Kathleen prefers not to leave her junking to fate. An avid dragger-home of chairs, tables, and lamps, she has become a brilliant tactical scavenger. Here is her strategy: Scope out the best neighborhood in which to hunt (Kathleen, a New Yorker, prefers artsy TriBeCa and SoHo, where wealthy artists abandon their wares). Find out which day of the week the trash is collected; on that day, don a jogging suit, go to the neighborhood, and look around. When you find a treasure, take it home in a cab. Kathleen's method is perfect: She gets either a workout or a find. Either way, her hard work pays off.

"HOW TO SUCCEED IN LEASING WITHOUT REALLY TRYING": SUBLETS, HOUSESITTING, AND OTHER WAYS TO AVOID SIGNING A LEASE

"TO BE COMMITTED IS TO BE IN DANGER."

—JAMES BALDWIN

If you've moved to the city on a whim, signing a yearlong lease may be more of a commitment than you're willing to make. You can put your toe in the water that is your city of choice, and save yourself money and grief, by keeping your name off a lease. There are several ways of doing this.

Sublets

One way to nibble at urban life is to get a sublet. Some of the best apartments are found through sublets. When people want to keep their pieds-à-terre in their names, but are unable to live in their city of choice for a set period of time, subletting is often their only option. Sublets are also ideal for those times when the lease of your own apartment runs out before you've decided on your next living situation. They can buy you time while you find a livable situation, or advance to your next plan. The terms vary from situation to situation—from a monthlong let to one as long as a year, maybe even with the chance to renew. Some apartments come fully furnished, and some sublet situations allow for the temporary tenant to take over the lease if the inhabitant decides to relinquish it. If you're lucky, you may be able to hook up with an apartment in a rent-stabilized building. Or you may find that during your three-month stay, moving to that particular city was the dumbest decision you ever made, and you can skip town without having to cover your tracks.

Housesitting

There are people who've never had to settle down with a lease, or a sublet for that matter, because they win the trust of long-term traveling types. Often, trusting travelers hand over their apartments or houses for a few weeks, a month, a year, and ask in return that the housesitter collect their mail, water the plants, and make sure nobody breaks into their homes. Experienced housesitters can coast from one such gig to the next for months, maybe even years, at a time. While this job is difficult to come by, housesitting is a wonderful cure for homelessness and beats the hell out of living at your parents' place. The people who need housesitters are often well off, so you can live large and you don't have to pay a dime. All in all, housesitters score big, as plant maintenance is about as hard as it gets.

Hermit Crabbing

Looking for an apartment is bad enough, but having to find roommates as well is double trouble. If you want to remain leaseless, find a ready-made household. Emulate the shrewd habits of the hermit crab, who, having no home of his own, simply moves into others' shells. Many people are looking for that third roommate because their previous roommate decided to move in with his girlfriend of two weeks or move back in with the 'rents. If you walk this road, you may get your own room, get to watch the roommates' TV, use their cookware, and listen to their CDs. You need only contribute your share of the rent—sans the startup costs of an apartment—and everything can be yours. Why? Because your roommates are so relieved to have you there, filling the financial void left by that reckless predecessor. And, because your name isn't on the lease, if you are reckless as well, it is easier to leave if you decide the housing situation doesn't suit your needs.

Loft Spaces

While lofts aren't necessarily lease-free, they are usually intended for industrial use rather than domestic living, so the agreement you sign may not be a formal lease: You will be living there as an illegal subletter. But don't let the term *illegal* scare you off. If you have Bob Villa tendencies, this could be your key to having that dream home. Sometimes lofts have already been domesticated by the previous tenants, but more often than not, the work is in your hands, and if you have the time and the talent, this could be well worth it. (For specifics, refer to the Profile: Lofty Living, page 35).

Carpetbagging

The simplest and cheapest way to avoid signing a lease is not to get an apartment. Living out of a bag reduces survival to its lowest common denominators: toothbrush and underwear. Your friends have beds and sofas; they have spare towels, toothpaste, and shampoo; they have everything you need, including the companionship you'd seek of them even if you had a place to live. If you have a constitution strong enough to relinquish your materialism, sample this liberating style of scrimping. Be careful, however, to take some precautions: (1) Like sharks, carpetbaggers must keep moving in order to stay alive. Don't stay longer than a few consecutive days at one apartment. (2) Like soldiers, they must have a strategically located storage facility at which they can replenish supplies. Usually, this is a parents' home in a nearby suburb. (3) Like Hollywood agents, they must have lots of contacts and be shameless about using them. You need to line up as many couches as you can, so get on the phone and start dealing.

Profile

Lofty Living

Pamela

Pamela has lived in New York City all of her life. Her parents raised her in an Upper East Side townhouse, and though Pamela has lived everywhere from Massachusetts to France, she always ends up back in the Bad Apple. After having spent a year on the top floor of her parents' house, Pamela decided to settle in NYC, but she needed to sever the umbilical cord. She scored the loft of her dreams, for obnoxiously low rent, in Queens. As a painter, Pamela needed this space, a possible tax write-off. But, it wasn't quite ready yet. Never fear. Our heroine helped enough friends move, welcomed enough folks to her couch for weeks at a time. It was time to cash in the chips. Mom and Dad were in no rush to have her move out—after all, help like her didn't come by too easily. Pamela signed the lease, crashed down the walls, and reconstructed a beautiful home and studio to her taste with a little help from her friends—all of them. True, she didn't move in until four months into her lease, but for the rent she was paying, it was well worth the investment. As Burt Bacharach wrote, "this house is now a home/this house became a home."

Beth

Beth is a sculptor with a carpentry background who focuses her work on major installations. A year after completing her MFA, a school in San Francisco offered her a tenure-track position to teach art, and with that she ventured westward to sort out her new living situation. She needed to find a place that would at once house her, her motorcycle, and her tremendous artwork. Loft living had to be the answer to her prayers. She moved into a warehouse of lofts, home to the Bay Area art scene, and began building a two-floor metropolis. When she first moved in, the space was completely empty: no bathroom, no kitchen, and a communal toilet facility down the hall of the building. The loft measured five hundred square feet, with ceilings reaching higher than the sun, and six hundred dollars a month rent. Our heroine built a state-of-the-art kitchen, a full bathroom complete with a spacious linen closet, a gigantic work space, a second-floor living room, a study with built-in bookcases, and a bedroom. She hoisted up her large installation pieces and suspended them from the ceiling, leaving herself enough work space to create even more. The loft metamorphosed into a hot bachelorette pad, where luxurious bathing and elaborate dinner parties were added to the creator's repertoire.

Profile

WiNɢ ANd A PRAYER

JOAN

Joan had just finished her master's degree in Baltimore, and after having deferred adult life for three years, she wasn't quite ready to embrace a definitive metropolitan plan of action. She dropped in on the District of Columbia one day, made a few calls from the local Howard Johnson's, and landed a three-month sublet in a one-bedroom. Two and a half months into the sublet, Joan was smart enough to think ahead, and persuaded a friend who was about to embark on a four-month European business exchange to let Joan sublet her place at a negligible rate. At the end of six months of sub-letted living in D.C., Joan was growing tired of living in the nation's capital, and her job wasn't too satisfying. She followed up on a job contact in Philadelphia, and was soon mastering the art of living out of a bag for a month at a time and sleeping on her college room-mate's couch for several weeks in that historic city. As she became in-volved with her college chum's housemate, she extended the stay in the apartment a bit longer, moved into his bedroom, until she even-tually scored a yearlong sublet in a neighboring building. Philly was falling into place for Joan, as she landed full and satisfying employment, a love interest, and a leaseless living arrangement with no sign up *letting* up.

Ed

Ed is a breath away from becoming a freeloader. The problem is, he is utterly charming, so for the purpose of this profile, we will call him a serial housesitter. After having spent the summer after college living with his parents in Boca Raton, he needed to find a home away from home, but wasn't willing to pay for one. He got a job waiting tables at a chichi restaurant in Miami, and between his regular clientele and the parents of childhood friends, Ed schmoozed his way into housesitting gigs for a month here, two weeks there, three months somewhere else, with only an occasional week or two using his parents' home as an interim residence. He was able to coast along this way for almost eight months, and just as he was about to exhaust his last contact, he fell fast in love with a fellow housesitter. The two decided to drive cross-country and work their Rolodexes up and down the West Coast. To this day, Ed has never paid rent for more than two months in a row, and presently resides with his girlfriend in Berkeley.

The Tele Box of Housing

If you think your housing situation is weird, take comfort in some of your favorite TV friends' living situations:

Three's Company The Ropers, landlords to Chrissy and Janet, are not keen on allowing a man to room with the girls in their three-bedroom. Jack Tripper does not want to pass up this great housing deal, so he pretends to be gay.

The Brady Bunch A gay man and a diva share a bed and read *Jonathan Livingston Seagull* every night. They pack six kids into two bedrooms with the help of only one bunk bed. Eventually the eldest son gets to move up to the attic to set up his hot bachelor pad, still leaving five kids to two rooms and one shared bathroom, with no toilet in sight!

Kate and Allie Two divorced women who are not sleeping together, and their children share a duplex.

Bosom Buddies Tom Hanks and Peter Scolari move to the big city with little money. They find a quaint little hotel for long-term residents whose rent ain't too shabby. There's only one problem: It is a women-only residence. The boys strap on breasts and wigs, and kick up their heels. Problem solved.

Sesame Street Big Bird squats behind an apartment building, and still has a houseguest management problem in Mr. Snuffleupagus, an unidentifiable creature who crashes in unexpectedly and leeches off his six-foot-tall feathered friend. Bert and Ernie live together, bathe together, and sleep together. Oscar the Grouch lives in a modest garbage can, which would be listed in the classifieds as *spac. conv. 1-bdrm w/skylite.*

The Mary Tyler Moore Show Our beloved news producer's studio apartment is a gem, but it is a studio nonetheless, and MTM sleeps on a sofabed.

Laverne & Shirley Two swingin' single gals who work together in a Milwaukee brewery share a basement apartment without a deadbolt, enabling wacky neighbors Lenny and Squiggy to constantly surprise them.

Happy Days Hipster of his day, Arthur Fonzarelli, known to most as "the Fonz," scores an apartment: a room over the garage of a rosy-cheeked all-American family.

Mork & Mindy An alien moves into the attic. This one is from a planet where it is acceptable to wear suspenders over a brightly colored, horizontally striped crewneck shirt. Planet *Zoom?*

Scooby Doo The whole gang, including the dog, seem to be living out of their van, the Mystery Machine. Glamorous bohemian detectives or slacker draft-dodging hippies? You decide.

The Monkees The band lives in an expensive bungalow with a spiral staircase. An example of why you shouldn't overextend yourself even for a dreamy duplex with stained-glass windows. The rent is split four ways, and the boys are still in constant dire straits.

The Odd Couple Sportswriting slob Oscar Madison and neatnik control freak Felix Unger move in together after their respective divorces. The apartment is grand, but the difference between roommates, irreconcilable.

MI CASA, SU CASA: DEALING WITH HOUSEGUESTS

"SOME PEOPLE CAN STAY LONGER IN AN HOUR THAN OTHERS CAN IN A WEEK."

—W. D. HOWELLS

If you are living in a city, your apartment—no matter what its size—will be a beacon for bored suburbanites gunning for hotel-free metropolitan adventures. Sometimes having houseguests is fun: You get to see old friends in a childhood-reprise, sleepover setting. You get to eat with them, hang out, chat, rent movies, show them the town, and expect a returned favor the next time you have a few vacation days (see I Was Just in the Neighborhood: Visiting Friends, page 153). But there is a fine line between a breezy sojourner and a barnacle. Seize the reins of hosting with skillful confidence, and you'll be rewarded with guests who move in and out of your apartment with graciousness and fluidity.

The Size of Your Apartment Is Directly Proportionate to the Amount of Time Guests Can Expect to Stay

If you have a studio, a holiday weekend is the limit of a polite visit. In a one-bedroom, one week. Two bedrooms, two weeks. Three bedrooms (and generous roommates), three weeks. Three weeks is stretching it in any size apartment unless the visitor is (1) a very close, nearly invisible friend, (2) having sex with you during her stay, or (3) from overseas.

Too Long a Sacrifice Can Make a Stone of the Heart

Heed Yeats's words. You don't want to spend a friendship-threatening length of time entertaining that long-lost college pal who has just moved to town to hunt for an apartment. Set limits. Let the guest know that the arrangement is temporary because in just three weeks you have to (1) move all the furniture into the kitchen to have the floors refinished; (2) entertain your brother and his friends who are spending their spring break/winter break/weekend furlough from jail with you; or (3) explain to the co-op board why you've been violating the terms of your lease.

Deadlines are rarely necessary for out-of-town friends who have jobs to return to. Then it's just a matter of endurance. If you are concerned, ask to see the return ticket.

Use It or Lose It

Put the houseguest to work. Most houseguests welcome this; they like to repay your generosity with simple gestures you recommend. Houseguests are perfect for feeding the cat, waiting around for UPS packages, letting in the cable guy, and washing dishes.

Double Your Pleasure

Let your vacationing houseguest know that it's absolutely fine if he brings his friend or lover along for the pull-out couch trip at your place. Although entertaining two sounds more daunting than one, it's actually easier. Each of the pair will entertain the other, leaving you with more time on your hands. And because your friend will have other company, you won't have to visit the Bunker Hill Monument or the Liberty Bell for the billionth time. You can stick to showing your guest the Boston or Philly that tourists never see— the right bars, the cozy restaurants—and do things you'd be doing anyway.

Passing Fancy

Houseguests make ideal one- or several-night stands. They have genuine affection for you and no delusions of commitment. As the party with the home court advantage, the host should ideally be the person to make the first move. Houseguests can make passes too, of course, but they must be careful. After all, they are the ones that really stand to lose (a place to sleep) if things go awry. If you are a houseguest and want to make a pass, be sure to feel the host out before you feel her up.

Note: *Matters are complicated by roommates. Set a policy. How long can folks stay? Can guests borrow the beds of absent roommates? How many stragglers can you take in at once? Remember: Houseguests come and go, but roommates usually stay until the end of the lease.*

Profile

BE (NOT) MY GUEST

SHARON AND DAVID

Sharon and David have been married for four years. When they moved to New York City, houseguests declared it open season at their apartment. Sharon's North Carolinian relatives, David's Irish ones, friends from college, friends from graduate school, friends of the family: Marital bliss was marred by a parade of houseguests in the couple's one-bedroom, one-bath apartment.

Some guests were demure and respectful, others brash and inconsiderate. Sharon quickly realized the crucial difference between the tolerable guests and the intolerable. Some guests were visiting Sharon and David and others were just using their apartment as a free Howard Johnson's during their vacations in the big city. Sharon figured out a way to dramatically reduce the congestion. If someone asked to "visit you and David" for a few days, fine. If someone asked to "crash on the couch," sorry.

MARTHA

Martha first moved to a major city when she was twenty-three. Her friends back south boasted that she was the one to get out of suburban hell. She moved into a two-bedroom, inheriting an older female roommate. There was a small annex room the size of a twin-size futon off of Martha's bedroom, which she used as a guest room. The prouder her friends became of her, the more frequently they visited to display that pride. Martha's dear friend Mark decided to have an urban vacation in the annex room, and never left. His boyfriend came by to visit the two, and he never left either. While it didn't bother Martha too much, the roommate was not amused, and the three were left in search of a new home. Until they found one, the boys continued to squat in Martha's new place rent free, but they showed their gratitude as her live-in house maintenance staff, providing gourmet cooking and immaculate cleaning from bathroom to litterbox. Martha brought home the bacon, the boys fried it up in a pan, washed the dishes, wiped down the tables, and swept the floors, and the three lived happily ever after . . . for a year's time.

ShoppiNq

Getting and Spending, We Lay Waste Our Power

"DO WHAT YOU CAN, WITH WHAT YOU HAVE, WHERE YOU ARE."

—TEDDY ROOSEVELT

In order to lead a frugally indulgent life, it is imperative that you learn to shop properly. What you buy and what you choose *not* to buy trumpet to the world who you are. Shopping is like learning a language: In order to be really fluent you've got to practice often, learn the drills, and get out there and live it. Follow us.

Learn and obey these seven habits of highly effective shoppers:

1. *Read.* Yes, it requires discipline to look at all your junk mail, catalogs, newspapers, and magazines, as well as their ads, but you must keep current—on fashion, sales, deals, designers, openings, closings, and so on. You should be reading a wide variety of material (refer to Cultured Pearls of Wisdom, on page 101), but as far as clothing is concerned (which you will learn is the most essential of the shopping genres) *Vogue* and *Harper's Bazaar* are crucial. Not only does magazine perusal keep you posted on style, it gives you details: dates, times, and prices. Clip notices of sales you want to re-

member and record them on your calendar. Ads for sales are invitations; treat them respectfully.

2. *Receive lots of catalogs.* Catalogs give you advance notice of sales, providing coupons and shopping opportunities. Get your name on all the mailing lists you can. This is easy. Companies like Tweeds and Pottery Barn sell your name and address to similar companies—you'll find that promotional mail breeds like bunnies. Put your name and address on catalog sign-up sheets in shops. Apply for every store credit card available. The stores automatically add your name to their mailing lists (and usually give you 10 percent off your first purchase). Shopping is no place to be a snob (save that for dating): You ought to receive every catalog, from Neiman Marcus to Lillian Vernon to Orvis. You never can tell what will turn up.

3. *Shop at every opportunity you get.* Given that you have no money, this may sound like telling an alcoholic to frequent bars, but bear with us. Shopping with no money, window shopping, browsing—call it what you will—is the intellectual equivalent of reading. It keeps you up-to-date, telling you what's in, when the sales will take place, which prices are reasonable, whose sales staff is bitchy, and so on. Go shopping (not buying, mind you; we'll get to that in a moment) as often as you can. Do not restrict your browsing to shops in which you really may buy something. Go to Versace, YSL, Pierre Deux, and the like, as well as midlist shops like Anne Taylor and Banana Republic, discount houses (T.J.Maxx and Marshalls), and delightfully divey thrift stores. Don't just window shop—go inside and try things on. Don't let the staff intimidate you. They are probably just as badly paid as you are. (They get those clothes and housewares at cost.) You'll be able to talk authorita-

tively on trends and you'll know what to look for when it comes time to getting it for less elsewhere. Browsing is like going to an art gallery: Most of the merchandise is too expensive for you to think of owning it, but it's nice that they let you look at it, and in the case of shopping, try it on. Do it at lunch, on the way home from work, or in full force on the weekends. It is entertaining and usually inexpensive (because persuals will far outnumber actual purchases), and that's reason enough for you to dig in your heels.

4. *Buy only a few items at a time.* Shopping frequently encourages you to buy a little here, a little there. This is good. Don't go on shopping sprees; you'll spend all your acorns in one place and may have to suffer a long winter without the tiniest morsel of indulgence. An awful prospect.

5. *Always pay with credit.* Cash (and checks) are inconvenient. Buy items with your store credit card if you'll get an extra discount; otherwise use your frequent flyer–earning credit card (see Frugal Finance, page 186).

6. *Put the crystal on the table; wear the jacket now.* There is nothing worse than indulging in a delicious extravagance only to leave it in the box because it is too nice to be used regularly. Remove the crystal from the cupboard, the jacket from the closet. You bought them to show them off, right?

7. *Chin up.* Let's dip into cliché for a moment and remember that happiness can't be bought in a shop. (And if it could, you probably couldn't afford it.) Money stifles creativity. It doesn't take *savv* to drape a person or apartment with finery for a king's ransom. Manifested in plummy housewares, Bouviessent clothing, and a swanky lifestyle, your cleverness will overshadow your shabby salary. Once more into the breach, dear friends!

THE SHOPPING QUIZ

1 It's lunch on a sunny Friday. You've had a shitty week. Your lunch date has canceled and your boss is out that day, leaving you time to kill. You have fifteen dollars setting your palm on fire. You must indulge, but in what?

a. a swell lunch by yourself
b. a CD
c. lipstick
d. pleather mules
e. nothing; you will save that fifteen dollars for a rainy Friday

2 It's your best friend's birthday. You know that she spent thirty dollars on your present last year; you don't even spend thirty on your parents. What to do?

a. Make a tape and present it with a bouquet of flowers.
b. Invite her for a dinner Chez You.
c. Go to the department store and buy thirty dollars' worth of whatever.
d. Go to a novelty or thrift store and buy a trinket relating to an inside joke for inside ten dollars.
e. Send a pretty card with nice sentiments and false promises within.

3 Which of the following credit cards are in your name?

a. Visa
b. MasterCard

c. American Express
d. Discover
e. Sears Roebuck
f. Macy's/Marshall Field's/Filene's, etc.
g. Barneys/Saks Fifth Avenue/Neiman Marcus, etc.
h. Exxon/Mobil/Amoco/Texaco, etc.
i. AT&T
j. Nobody Beats the Wiz/Lechmere

4 Grandpa Sam has you visit his pad in Fort Lauderdale for a week. His retired city buddies are enthralled by little besides golf, leaving you to your own devices. You can take only so much of lying by the poolside watching children float around in their Power Rangers inflatable tubes. You venture to the nearest Goodwill, and find a mint-green Courrèges trench coat, beautifully tailored with hand-sewn snaps, its removable lining intact, for ten dollars. The sleeves, however, fall a bit short, not to mention the fact that you've already spent too much attempting to entertain yourself with margaritas, dinners, and movies, and have sworn that you wouldn't spend another dime during your last two days. Despite the fact that this coat is neither your color nor your exact fit, you feel this offer is too good to refuse. You:

a. toss your promise to yourself out the window and buy the damn thing
b. leave the store at once, go get a margarita to ponder the potential purchase, and muster up the courage to return to the store in a few hours to recontemplate
c. leave the store and try to forget you ever saw the coat

5 It has finally come to pass: That person you've been ogling has finally invited you out for a chichi dinner on Saturday night. While you are beside yourself with glee, the anxiety begins to

set in as you try to subdue your glamorexic tendencies: You have nothing resembling fabulous to wear. In order to keep your swellegance in check, you:

a. raid your best friend's closet
b. rush over to the Betsey Johnson boutique, and drop a load of credit on a Vreelandish little sale item that you will probably wear only once
c. get creative with the local vintage shops, and put together an outfit that screams classic and timeless
d. suggest a more casual evening so you can wear that same tired (unlucky) little number you love so much
e. pull a Grace Jones and wear only a fur—nudity never goes out of style

6   You've just moved into your first studio apartment, almost a year to the day since you landed your first serious job. While in addition to your own place you have a ratty futon, three chipped plates, a dessert fork, a serrated knife, a soup spoon, and a bookcase, your abode is a bit too humble. Luckily, your beloved and generous Aunt Phyllis celebrates the commencement of your new "real" life by sending you a three-hundred-dollar gift certificate from Crate & Barrel (we should all have an Aunt Phyllis). Where to begin?

a. a wicker chair ($120); a beige sisal 6x9 rug ($75); a folding bookcase ($60); a wooden dish rack ($15); 2 clay pot–bound candles ($15 a pop) = $300
b. a complete set of bedsheets ($80); a set of four bath towels ($70); an aquarium-print shower curtain ($20); a shaker rug ($18); a wrought-iron soap dish ($15); a colored-glass toothbrush container ($12); and a reversible vanity mirror ($25) = $240
c. a reversible bookcase ($90); a Bodum Bistro coffeemaker ($40);

a set of 6 votive candles in wrought-iron case with glass interior ($32); 2 martini glasses, 2 white wine glasses, 2 red wine glasses, 2 champagne flutes ($48); and a bedspread on sale ($110) = $320

d. plateware for 4 ($60); flatware for 4 ($55); a set of 4 tumblers, each a different color ($20); a tea kettle ($35); a director's chair with slipcover ($80); a night lamp ($50) = $300

ANSWERS

1. If you chose **c,** give yourself four points. That lipstick will go a long way, baby, and give you and the others who look you straight in the lips infinite joy. Three points for choosing the CD. While it doesn't afford the instant gratification lipstick does (unless you brought your CD Walkman to lunch), this has lasting power too, and will entertain you for hours at a time on repeat play. Two points for lunch. Sometimes you have to splurge, and let's face it, food is a comfort. But lunch has more calories than lipstick, and its only lasting effect is heartburn and cellulite. One point for choosing **e** and saving it, and a big pat on the back for endurance. There is the risk you may snap later and indulge, but kudos for taking it one day at a time. Zero for pleather. *Hint: Pleather is never acceptable in any situation.*

2. If you chose **b,** take four points. Inviting someone to your home is intimate, and people are always impressed by a reasonably well executed meal. It will probably set you back thirty dollars anyway, but you get to share, and there may be leftovers for lunch. Three points for making a tape (**a**). Lots of thought, time, and personal knowledge of someone's taste goes into making a tape. Flowers brighten any day. You will be on your friend's mind

every time she listens to the tunes and stares at the posies. Two points for **d.** A close second to **a,** jokes require thought and acknowledge intimacy, but the actual retail value will be apparent. One point for a thoughtless thirty-dollar present. You're out the cash and you've bought with less creativity and love than is possible in some other choices. Cheesy cards and false promises don't bode well.

3. Give yourself a point for each credit card in your name except AmEx. Award yourself three points for each credit card that gives you frequent flyer miles unless that card has an annual fee, in which case award yourself only one point. Deduct five points if you have AmEx in your name. Add five points if you have AmEx in your company's name (expenseploitation!). We don't promote credit cards that expect one to pay the balance in full at the end of the month, nor do we encourage membership with an annual fee; hence, AmEx is a no go.

4. There is only one correct answer for this question: You must buy bargain designer thrift items on sight. The size, the color scheme—these things are irrelevant. It is Courrèges, darling, and even elderly Floridians at a Goodwill know quality when they see it. *Someone else will seize it if you don't.* Remember, a find is a terrible thing to waste. Four points for choosing the correct answer. Subtract five points for **b** or **c.**

5. You get four points for getting creative (**c**). Classic and timeless is as Bouviessent as it gets. You look fabulous for your date, and glambidextrous when you use it again somewhere down the line. This is not to say that indulging in the Vreelandish sector shouldn't be commended. Give yourself three points for knowing when to splurge. True, you won't be able to wear it in coming seasons, but you may extend its fashion existence for a few extra months by

throwing a blazer over it. Two points for those who have friends with closets worthy of raiding. Only one point for downscaling the evening (**d**)—that outfit never worked for you before, and it certainly won't on Saturday. As for **e**, do you actually know anyone who could wear nudity like Grace? Didn't think so. No points, for lack of reality.

6. The rule of found money such as a gift certificate is as follows: Indulge to the max. This is your invitation; R.S.V.P. with relish. Bearing that in mind, if you've chosen **c,** you win three points. Savor the gratification of having the chance to buy all those things you don't need but must have. Sure, you've gone over the limit, but think of it this way: You got all that for only twenty dollars (not to mention that great deal you got on the bedspread!). Two points for **d** if you like to entertain, one point if you don't. How can you entertain in a studio apartment? If you've figured out a means, you may give yourself the greater reward. Note: Frugal Indulgents don't buy chairs; they acquire them, be it on a street corner, as an inheritance from a former roommate/tenant, or for pennies from the Salvation Army. If you don't like to entertain in the kitchenette, two points for the bathroom/bed set (**b**), but you've left money in the till. Oh, well, if that's your way, we suppose you can use that sixty dollars next season. This selection buys you vanity space with style. Otherwise, award yourself one point, as you probably don't need that many towel and sheet collections—you don't want to encourage houseguests to stay with you in your two-room apartment for more than a night. Attention: You do not get points for wicker (**a**)—leave it in the showroom and on the deck. Like that rose tattoo, you'll regret getting it in a year.

THREADS ON A SHOESTRING: CLOTHES, ACCESSORIES, COSMETICS

"FASHION FADES—STYLE IS ETERNAL."

—YVES SAINT LAURENT

Clothing is the most important thing money can buy. You can hide a shabby apartment; you can pretend you are not in the mood for four-star food; you can feign boredom at the notion of an Italian holiday, but you cannot pretend that you don't like looking fabulous. It just wouldn't make sense.

There are several basic strategies to bear in mind as you build and maintain your wardrobe, the most important of which follows Polonius's sage advice to Laertes: "To thine own self be true." In other words—those of Diana Vreeland—"Once you find your look, stick to it." Clothing represents your personality; it tells people a lot about you. Don't confuse colleagues and loved ones by wearing a schizophrenic wardrobe. They will imagine that you are as volatile as your closet.

Choosing a collection whose pieces complement one another is crucial for another reason: It keeps your wardrobe to a manageable size and makes it easier to match the few things you do have. Vintage items look swell with other vintage items; likewise for classic new pieces. (However, a foolish consistency remains the hobgoblin of little minds: If that brand-new Nehru jacket will look dashing over your circa 1950 floral housecoat—unlikely, but let's pretend—by all means, indulge.)

Consider these suggestions as you cultivate your collection:

- *Throw it away.* When you don't have much, it can be difficult to part with what you do have. You may find that, like a war-era grandmother who clings to bits of string, you hang on to clothing too long for no good reason. Clean out your closet often. You are better off wearing a spiffy pair of trousers several times a week (so long as it doesn't have an assertive print) than risking making an appearance as a *dumpster,* in a threadbare or, worse yet, unfashionable pair. The clothing that remains when you weed out the duds—uglies, worn-outs, and never-wears—will have more space to hang wrinkle free. Call the Salvation Army or take rejects to a consignment shop—just get them out of the apartment.

■ *Take care of what you have.* Once you have a well-selected wardrobe of choice garments, take care of them. Things last a long time in good condition when you dry clean, hand wash, hang dry, and iron. Do your own laundry if possible, rather than dropping it off. Laundromats ruin things. A year later your T-shirts will have stretched a size larger and faded a color lighter. Underwear waistbands? Shot to hell. If you want laundry done right, bring a magazine and do it yourself. When in doubt, dry clean. Dry cleaning is an indulgence you should enjoy. Frequent dry cleaning encourages the frequent wearing of fabulous fabrics like wool and linen. You are all grown up now; dry cleaning helps wean you from your all-cotton college diet. Think of dry cleaners as pawnshops; if you don't have the money to pick up your clothes when they're ready, simply leave them in hock until your next paycheck arrives.

■ *Get a good tailor.* This is key to keeping things in good condition, as well as upgrading imperfect finds. As soon as you get a run, hole, snag you can't fix yourself but think is reparable, bring it to your tailor. A good tailor will work reasonably priced wonders. If you find a gorgeous two-hundred-dollar dress at T.J.Maxx for forty-five dollars in size ten and you are a size eight, you can buy it with confidence. The tailor will alter it for seventy-five dollars or so. At first, it may seem hard to justify paying more for a few tucks than you did for the garment itself, but you'll get used to it when you consider the big economic picture. You've saved eighty dollars and essentially ended up with a custom-made garment.

▪ *Dress up rather than down.* The old tenet for dressing, that you should err on the side of formality, goes for buying as well. Buy up, not down. Of course you've got to have play clothes too, but when you are assembling your wardrobe, try to select things that will do double duty. Many shirts, when a blazer is thrown over them, travel fluidly from office to dive bar.

▪ *Indulge.* When was the last time you bought a garment other than a winter coat that cost more than a hundred and twenty dollars? Isn't it time to commit Salvation Armani? Treat yourself every now and then to a fabulous big-ticket extravagance. So you'll eat rice and beans for a few months—isn't it worth it to wear glamour on your sleeve?

When you step out to indulge, leave recklessness and impulse at home. Don't buy something too trendy, too showy, or too dressy. Trendy will fall out of fashion; showy and dressy won't suit as many occasions as you hope. Select something utterly elegant but understated. You may think that nobody will notice a pair of Donna Karan cigarette pants, a long black YSL skirt, a basic leather belt from Coach, a pair of Prada heels, but they will. Quality speaks volumes in a whisper.

Decadence and whimsy are grand companions. Now you can afford to couple one plum item with a trashy one. A gorgeous pair of trousers upgrades the look of a brassy ten-dollar sale shirt. The bold irony in the cheap find is offset by the tastefulness evident in the trousers. Your style is considered *and* daring.

Note: *If you are not entirely confident with your indulgence, leave it hanging on your bedroom door or in your closet with the tags on for a few days. Does it look like it belongs? Can you really give it the attention it deserves? Are your*

*friends and roommates envious? If the answers are yes, it does, yes, I can, yes,
then keep it. If not, it's back to Bergdorf's.*

Making the [Wo]Man: Clothes

When Adam and Eve were evicted from the Garden of Eden, they
knew that the fig leaves were just an act of making do. Their scanty
outfits of nature would never ride the groove train of fashion outside
of the Garden. Banishment gave the first couple a ticket to couture
paradise. Suddenly, the first question on their minds was, what
should we wear? Casual attire? Formal? Classic? Trendy? The two
winked at each other, and embarked on their first shopping expedi-
tion.

Your time has come. You can't always depend on those clothes
you got the summer before you went to college. You are an adult
now, and it is time to get your look together.

Before you make your entrance into a store, you must assess the
options. When is it appropriate to buy vintage? Retail? Simulacra-
wear? This is a very subjective question, one only you can answer
based on your sense of savv and self.

We've created a chart to aid in your contemplation process. You'll
find that you may have to commit the occasional Salvation Armani,
and pick up a few accessories to be inducted to the world of the decadencia. You don't want to overdo it, however—you don't need to
have credit card bills putting you out for the next twenty years. It is
utterly humiliating to return from a shopping experience to find an
empty wallet and a quasimode look—it often costs more money to
be a breath away from fashionable than to hit the fashion nail right
on the head. To help you understand, we've divided clothing items
into three categories: *vintage,* which constitutes any clothes with a
previous history; *retail,* anything bought new, be it on sale or not (we,
of course, prefer the former); and *simulacra-wear* (Gap-like basics for
which there is no original).

Clothing Item	Vintage	Retail	Simulacra-Wear
Basic Black Dress	If you can find one, grab it. (It may be just as easy and cost as much to buy new.)	It is always acceptable to commit Salvation Armani for a basic black dress. Go to Barneys, Bergdorf's, Bendel's, a boutique—one should never scrimp on a necessity of life. Think of this as an investment, as this dress provides years of satisfaction.	It may be basic, it may be black, but it is an investment. You want it to have some original character, which you won't find here.
Jeans	If you think that wearing the Levi's with another's history is sexy, by all means, make the purchase. There is something comforting in having broken-in jeans caressing your inner thighs, but recall that former sex god Marlon Brando may have worn those for a week, sans undies, to prepare for *Streetcar*. Some find that sexy, others find it as repulsive as prechewed food.	Spending eighty dollars plus on a new pair of Calvins seems wasteful. Don't you have a roommate, sibling, or ex-lover you can steal from? Save that money for shoes.	If there is one thing the Gap does right everytime, it is making jeans. Simulacra-wear in this instance is totally acceptable.

Clothing Item	Vintage	Retail	Simulacra-Wear
Two-piece suit	They don't make suits like they used to, save for those by Paul Smith, Giorgio Armani, Jean-Paul Gaultier, Calvin Klein, and the like. If you don't have that kind of money, vintage is the affordable way to purchase the timeless style offered by such suitsmiths.	If you have one thousand dollars lying around, waiting for the right suit, commit Salvation Armani; but do it wisely. *Frugalize your indulgence (FYI)* and pick a suit that you'll be able to wear for years to come. Also, if outlets are in your vicinity, try to get the best deal possible. You can save up to seven hundred dollars, without cramping your style.	Nothings screams dumpster like a nondescript suit from Sears. Don't waste any money on styleless threads, no matter how cheap. If you want to spend under $200 on a good suit, refer to the vintage option.
T-shirts, turtlenecks, plain dress shirts, and other cotton shirt basics			There is never a need to indulge on such necessities. These do not need to be exciting. They are fillers, so treat them accordingly. This is what simulacra-wear is made for.
Shoes	Shoes are one instance where a previous history is not appealing. Buying used shoes is not unlike chewing	Shoes often make the outfit. If you wear cheap shoes, you run the risk not only of looking like a quasi-	

Clothing Item	Vintage	Retail	Simulacra-Wear
Shoes (cont.)	a piece of Dentyne that has been through the wash.	mode, but of experiencing severe discomfort in your feet, shins, and back. Salvation Armani is always acceptable in the shoe department—you'll look fabulous and your body will thank you.	
Sweaters	There is nothing quite like spending ten dollars on a cashmere cardigan from the 1960s—a timeless item. You can never go wrong buying a preowned sweater.	It isn't always necessary to shell out major cash for a new sweater, but it can provide years of satisfaction. Dolce & Gabbana makes a killer angora sweater. If you feel you must indulge, then do. You'll have it for years.	Though buying a vintage sweater will provide savings and years of satisfaction, a simple, simulacra sweater isn't the biggest faux pas. Shops like the Gap have a nice array of turtleneck, crewneck, and V-neck sweaters. If you hold out until your birthday or the gift-giving season, chances are family members will buy you one.
Jackets/Coats	If it is leather or suede, always buy used. There is nothing more flavorless than a new leather coat, except maybe unprewashed, new blue jeans. Wool coats, blazers, and jackets are always a thrift score, as well.	For cold climates, it is necessary to buy a new down coat. If you want wool or camel hair, it is best—economically—to go the vintage route.	

Closet Cases

There are as many ways to shop as there are people who do it. These samples offer just a few of the ways our friends have found to tame the wild clothes horse (or bring it to greener pastures):

On a reckless day, Lilian only buys clothing that is less than thirty dollars. She gets hand-me-downs from a friend who works at a department store and shops in discount retailers. She has lots of clothes and she wears things for years.

Jill uses the European model. She owns a few well selected, expensive pieces of clothing—most of which are black, so they all match—and she wears them all the time.

Kathleen is a fan of suburban discount stores and sample sales, but occasionally breaks down and commits Salvation Armani. When she splurged on a suit at Barneys, she told her friends to get used to it—they'd be seeing a lot of it.

Justin shops on the bargain racks of high-end retailers. He buys for January in July and vice versa. Shopping off-season ensures that everything he buys is marked Final Sale.

Vikash dislikes shopping. A few times a year, however, he drags himself to Brooks Brothers, where he buys the suits he needs. If he needs anything else, he refers to his catalogs—Lands' End, L.L. Bean, J. Crew—and phones in the order. He is never overcome with giddy delight when he shops; shopping is strictly business, and his ability to buy only what he needs ensures that he keeps the costs low.

Kerry's wardrobe features vintage items that she finds at a steal. No chance of her turning up in the same Gap dress as the rest of the gang. Everything she owns says "one-of-a-kind."

Profile

SCAVENGER HUNT

Jeff

As with many of us, Jeff's needs exceed his means. He deals cleverly (if not always scrupulously) with that reality. One weekend he spent in Boston he popped into Filene's Basement and bought a pair of white Armani jeans. The garment was lovely, but Jeff, *toujours au courant,* realized it was out of season. He removed the Filene's tag, dressed up well but casually and went to Armani Exchange when he returned home to New York City. In his most bored, nonchalant voice he explained to the clerk that the jeans were a gift and that they were all wrong for him. He traded them in for the newest model of black Armani jeans. The bottom line: If your morals are as loose as Jeff's, you can set your creativity loose at the nearest T.J.Maxx or Filene's Basement.

A caveat: What goes around may come around. Jeff brought the new Armani jeans to Spain on a business trip and had them laundered at his hotel. They returned from the valet with a broken zipper.

Jody

In an act that would make the Better Business Bureau proud, Jody spotted an advertisement in the local paper that Bloomingdale's was offering free makeovers to customers who purchased any YSL new cosmetic product. Wasting no time, she ran to the nearest Bloomie's, made a beeline for the YSL table, and found the lipstick of her dreams. She bought it for eighteen dollars and asked the clerk when she could expect her free makeover.

The clerk informed Jody that the makeover was available only to those customers who had purchased more than sixty-five dollars' worth of cosmetics.

Never fear. Jody was fully armed with the Saturday paper, complete with advertisement, which said nothing of a price minimum.

"Oh, there must have been a misprint," offered the clerk.

"Shall I speak to the manager?" Jody countered.

The clerk smiled, emerged from behind the counter loaded with YSL products, and before you knew it, Jody had metamorphosed into a new and improved beauty.

The bottom line: Glamour is priceless, so don't pay for it if you don't have to.

John

John knows quality when he sees it. He knows it whether he spots it in the window of a Coach leather shop on Madison Avenue, or in a garbage Dumpster. One afternoon he brought his recycling to the basement of his apartment building and noticed a leather handle peeking out from a pile of trash. He pulled on the handle to uncover a black-leather Coach briefcase identical to his own, which he had purchased for several hundred dollars. The foundling was dirty and tired, but John knew that old leather had a certain patina that only added charm. He brought it upstairs, vacuumed its interior, buffed its exterior with the leather refinishing cream he'd bought for a few dollars, and gave it to his girlfriend.

You Must Indulge in This . . . How to Compromise the Creative Way

When you don't have it all and can't get it all, you have to get creative. Creativity is productivity.

Diana Vreeland said it best when she noted that "elegance is refusal." A happy circumstance for those of us who have no choice but to refuse some of the finer things. Knowing what to refuse is essential. There are some things about which you simply cannot compromise.

Can't Live Without	Can Live Without
VCR	cable TV
a black dress	a black catsuit
a good lipstick	eyeshadow
a pair of black heels	anything pleather
restaurant food	eat-at-home-alone food
daily newspaper	daily tabloid
Filofax	phone book
great hairdresser	a psychic friend
condoms	the pill
one near-and-dear sex toy	love
answering machine/voice mail	fax machine
smart glasses	contact lenses
neighborhood café	coffee machine
saucepan	tea kettle
wine glasses (red and white)	water glasses
long-distance calls made from the office	long-distance calls made from home
cigarettes	a gym membership
a diner	a matching dishware set

CDs	concerts
health insurance	a doctorate
Brita water filter	Evian

You may think we are contradicting ourselves here, but it is simply not so. For example, making yourself happy with a sex toy is infinitely more satisfying than love. *Vibratoramor vincit omnia!* (From the Latin, "vibrators conquer all.") When the Beatles sang, "Money can't buy me love," they should have followed up with the point that it *can* buy you a sexual aid.

Coffee is something you buy on the outside, like Jerry Seinfeld does. With a saucepan you can make tea, hot cocoa, soup, or one-cup coffee servings, and you don't have to buy filters, or waste one of your few electrical outlets. Besides, if you live alone, there is nothing more depressing than leftover coffee in the pot. With a saucepan, you aren't reminded of your solitude.

Health insurance is often provided by a job, and you can get five-dollar prescriptions for anything, from Xanax and Prozac to antibiotics. You may also scam a free pair of eyeglasses once a year.

With a doctorate, you may be able to get a job that you are way overqualified for—sans insurance, sans security—with the sole satisfaction of being highly educated.

You can drink water out of wine glasses, but you really shouldn't drink wine out of water glasses.

Since we must scrimp and save at times, we will do it with class, and do it wisely.

The Frugal Indulgent's Purse

If there is one quick way to find out a woman's psychic makeup, it is to browse through her bag. (All it takes to understand a man is one glance at his shoes.) Here is a cross section of the female Frugal Indulgent purse:

two lipsticks One of them is likely to be MAC, Bobbi Brown, Chanel, or some other decadent brand. The other may be a more inexpensive brand. If a Frugal Indulgent were stranded on a deserted island, this is the one cosmetic she would bring.

a passport She is always prepared for international travel. She does not carry a driver's license or a state-issued I.D.— that would allow her to get only as far as Canada.

two sets of house keys One set is for her apartment, and the other belongs to that friend whose tremendous loft she is housesitting.

a bottle of Advil Urban life can be such a headache, and the one thing that Frugal Indulgents cannot tolerate is pain.

credit cards She never knows when she may have to commit Salvation Armani.

two dollars cash, three subway tokens, some dimes, nickels, pennies A Frugal Indulgent should never leave the house without money. This should get her through the day—she can expenseploitate lunch and cab fare. Note: she does not have quarters in her purse—they're at home waiting for laundry day. Besides, she has memorized her calling card number, and she dials 1-800-COLLECT.

a Filofax She always needs to be armed with important phone numbers and dates. Stuffed with unpaid bills, her Filofax reminds her to pay the electricity bill this month and the phone bill next month. She doesn't have stamps, though—that's what jobs are for.

a toothbrush In case she doesn't make it home before work the next morning. Before going out for another night of wining, dining, and smoking, she really should brush the stink of alcohol, garlic, and nicotine off her tongue.

sunglasses Not necessarily used for eye protection from the sun, but for protection against glamourexia nervosa as she braves the walk of shame from the train, car, or taxi to her front door, after a rowdy evening that ended at 8:00 A.M.

a receipt from that "business" lunch Before she attaches it to her expense report, she remembers to write down her friend's boss's name so that she can call it a business expense.

a postcard for an invite-only Anna Sui sample sale Yes, the event is marked on the calendar in the Filofax, but this is just an additional reminder.

a complaint letter to a major airline Her service to L.A. was absolutely shoddy. Perhaps they will appease her with a free will-this-shut-you-up? flight.

a tic-tac box containing 3 tic-tacs, 3 Xanax It is hard to tell them apart in the box, but you can't go wrong either way.

a pen She won't be denied someone's phone number just because he may not have a business card.

a rolled-up issue of Entertainment Weekly For infauxmational purposes.

a ticket stub from an art-house film She has to remember to give it to her accountant for creative tax deduction purposes.

Chanel's Allure perfume sample No need ever to buy it. By the time she uses it up, she will be sick of the fragrance, and once more into the breach for a new scent.

matchbook from Bistro Très Chere In the revolving door, out with a matchbook.

Games Shoppers Play

Sometimes hunting and gathering bargains can be wearing. Don't ever get too serious about shopping. Remember, it's fun! If shopping has lost some of its luster for you, try these simple exercises to recapture your interest:

Pet the Bunny

Go to Neiman Marcus and try on the furs. Say you must discuss your prospective purchase with your husband but that you'll be back before the season in Gstaad starts.

Borrow'd Robes

Need a dress for just one night? Treat a distant boutique as your local library. Take out a dress on your credit card and return it the next day. Follow the advice you see on TV: Never let 'em see you sweat.

A Little Dab'll Do You

Before a big night on the town, don't spend your money on perfume. Swing by Bloomies, find the tester you feel is appropriate for your evening and take a dab.

SETTING THE TABLE: A GUIDE TO HOUSEWARES

What do you really need to buy besides shelter (in which category we include furniture) and clothing? Nothing *really*; you could survive and be perfectly fine, but you wouldn't be able to make a bowl of pasta or eat a pint of Häagen-Dazs on a whim. For occasions on which you'd like to do so—breakfast, lunch, cocktails, dinner—you need housewares, especially kitchenware.

There are obvious (and good) ways of getting housewares cheaply: Look for sales at Lechmere, drop by the Dansk outlet, swing by the kitchen section at T.J. Maxx. You can likely finesse your way through life without some things others might consider essential, so don't spend a fortune on mini muffin tins. Unless you're a Martha Stewart disciple, you ought to be able to take creative and inexpensive routes to acquiring all the housewares you need. Consider these tried-and-truly-cheap methods:

Marriage and Divorce

It is in the formation and dissolution of household unions (your own and those of others) that you have the best chance of getting great housewares for free.

GET MARRIED. In the apartment chapter we learn that shacking up is the easiest way to save money on rent. When it comes to acquiring housewares, the easiest thing to do is to get married. Williams-Sonoma does not have a living-together registry, so shacking up won't help you. Unless your lover has already got the goods, you're going to have to get married to get other people to buy you that complete Calphalon set.

TRICKLE DOWN. If you don't want to get married, consider cozying up to marrying friends. Many people have been living together already when they marry so they often have plates to discard when they upgrade to their bridal shower gifts. If you are a close enough friend that you will be on the receiving line at the wedding, there's a good chance you could also be on the receiving end of some decent hand-me-downs.

DIVORCE. When people divorce they don't want to eat off dishes that remind them of defeat. Neighbors, parents, friends—advise the divorcing couples you know that if there is any painful memory in the form of china, crystal, or silver (they usually keep the pots and pans) you can remove for them, you'll be glad to do it.

GET ROOMMATES. If you can't form a legal union that would create an influx of copper pots to your home, create a union based on the convenience of another person's cookware. When you are interviewing prospective roommates always make sure to ask what they'll be bringing to the relationship and to the kitchen.

REGISTER. Once upon a time you may have cried when you received practical gifts in lieu of toys on your birthday. Now the reverse should be true. Buy yourself the toys and make other people get you the practical stuff. The easiest way to ensure you'll get the proper model of the vacuum/mixer/power drill you have your heart set on is to register for it. When Mom calls to ask what you want for Christmas, tell her the people from Crate & Barrel, Bergdorf-Goodman, and Williams-Sonoma have that answer. Note: Don't sell yourself short by signing up for small things like utensils. As with restaurant food (See Eating Out, page 103), if someone else is buying, shoot for the big-ticket items.

Secondhand Isn't Second Best

You wouldn't believe the things people throw away—or give away for pennies in their garages every spring: copper pots, cast-iron skillets, vintage appliances, even Fiestaware. When searching for household items, do not overlook garage sales, thrift stores, trash day, and flea markets. Seconds are fabulous because (1) they often boast cool vintage styles, (2) the saying "they don't make 'em like they used to" is true of many things, like heavy duty blenders (check the wiring), and (3) housewares are usually the cheapest items at tacky thrift shops and yard sales.

If You Are Going to Do It at All, Do It Right the First Time

If you don't have time to comparison shop before you buy an appliance—with a hand mixer, for example, get the good model—go for the KitchenAid or the Black & Decker. The cheap models may look good to your checkbook, but they may end up emitting smoke into your cookie batter. Not worth it in the end: Kitchenware is worth investing in if you'll use it more than once. Don't skimp; splurge. (But remember to negotiate before you buy a big-ticket item. See Profile: The Boston Haggler, on page 75.)

Get Creative

As you acquire housewares, let your imagination run wild. Tacky decor turns your kitchen (and indeed, your whole apartment) into a kitsch-in. Plastic plates, technicolor fixtures, dated appliances that still work, and tiki mugs are great conversation pieces that, in the eyes of the world, turn your frugality into eccentric decadence. Just as the kitchen is not only for kitsch, the living room is not merely for living. Of course you can entertain yourself and others there, but it also serves as a showcase for your exquisite street corner finds. Remember: Where there's a wall, there's a way.

DECORATE WITH JUNK. Discarded items that can be used as decor are perfect for your price range and even more challenging to work with than secondhand stuff. Found a taxi cab door on the street? Replace your Doisneau poster with it. (Replace your Doisneau poster in any case.) Found a traffic cone that looked up for grabs (don't they all?)? Put a snake lamp in its hole and relish your new piece of living room furniture.

REASSIGN PURPOSES. Lamp shades too expensive? Create a cheap alternative with an aluminum collander. Don't want to commit to a wine glass rack just yet? An old bicycle wheel becomes an elegant fixture when suspended from the ceiling with flutes in its spokes. Think Christmas lights are only for fir trees in December? Hang them in the kitchen and bask in the warm glow. How about a set of freebie ashtrays from your favorite drugstore, perched atop an abandoned wooden spool once meant for electric wire now used as a coffee table? Your friend's old VW van may be long dead, but that removable bench seating makes for quite a funky couch, especially with the seat belts still intact. Don't let tradition inhibit your sense of where things really belong.

FIVE-AND-DIME IT. In the right setting, trashy stuff becomes elegant. It's all about context. Janice's Toulouse-Lautrec bath mat cost five dollars at a warehouse store and—believe it or not—makes her apartment look like Paris. Barb's plastic tamale Christmas lights were twelve dollars and worth every penny.

DO AN ARTIST FRIEND A FAVOR. Do you know a talented painter/photographer/designer who is frustrated because she has no place to store her wares? Offer to be her warehouse. She gains a storage space/gallery, you get to throw away your museum reproduction prints and never look back.

Whine All the Way to the Cellar

Complain to your parents that the tinny echo they hear on the other end of the phone is your voice bouncing off the walls of your barren apartment. Ask what happened to that swell furniture/dish set/ standing lamp whose cute Pucci pattern has come back in vogue since they bought it on their honeymoon thirty years ago. If you have suburban parents, chances are the item is still in the cellar. Return for a visit and make a beeline for the basement/garage/attic to pillage.

Profile

THE BOSTON HAGGLER

JENNIE

Jennie is shocked to hear of friends who pay full price for things without even trying to talk the merchant down. Jennie treats downtown Cambridge as her local souk; she buys only after she's made the merchant earn it. Here is the wisdom of her haggling ways.

- *Choose your target.* The right store: Go to a mom-and-pop hardware store, not Lechmere. Go to a boutique, not a chain store. Realize that in order to get a discount on most items, you must be speaking with someone with authority.

  The right items: You are not going to get a discount on a twenty-dollar toaster. You may get one on a hundred-and-twenty-dollar vacuum. No matter what kind of store you are in, it is only on the big-ticket items—furniture, electronics—that you can get in your best haggling. Employees are sometimes allowed to discount these expensive things, and they are eager to have you buy them because they get a commission.

- *Remember that everything is negotiable.* View price tags as suggestions.
- *Know your stuff.* When you've comparison shopped, you'll know if the merchant is in the ballpark or not and you'll be able to use the "I saw it at Macy's for fifty dollars less" line with confidence.
- *Talk to the merchant.* Even if you know exactly what you want, look around, get the merchant's advice—engage him. Act sincerely interested, but not too eager.
- *Ask what the real price is.* Laugh at his response.
- *Ask if they offer discounts for students/locals/journalists.* Pick a category you fit into and ask if there is a special discount for it.
- *Ask if there is a display model that is cheaper than a new model.*
- *Find damages on the item and ask if the price will be corrected for them.*
- *Play it up.* Remember, you're acting. It helps to pretend you are Italian to get into the rhythm and melodrama of your role. Gesture a lot, look at the heavens and whisper, "Dio mio" or "Madonna mia," involve your family, mention shame and pride, mention the friendship and trust you felt was forming between you and the merchant, then say you will buy it at another store where they are reasonable.
- *Be coy.* Pretend you are dating. Flirt a bit; play hard to get. Head for the door. If you are urged back in, return cautiously. Continue the negotiation. If the merchant lets you leave, return the next day. Resume the negotiation. Repeat.
- *If you can't get a discount, aim for a freebie or another item at a discount.* It helps to buy things at the same place and time if you use this tactic. Then you can use the line, "But I'm buying a mixer *and* a food processor. Can't you give me a break?"

Profile

Sole Custody

Scott

When Scott graduated from college, he moved to an apartment in Seattle with two of his friends. His roommates remarked that they had certain household necessities: a couch, table, chairs, pots and pans. The only thing they didn't have was tableware. Scott could have bought it at Lechters or Crate & Barrel, paying lots of money for plates that probably wouldn't have as much character as he'd like. He could have searched flea markets for delightful mismatched sets, but he's not a vintage sort. He casually mentioned to his mother that he needed to buy a set of dishes. She told him not to: He could have the wedding china that had been languishing in her cellar since she and Scott's father divorced. That year, Scott and his roommates ate their rice and beans on gilt bone china.

Profile

The Rabble-Rouser

Lilian

"IF YOU DON'T GO OUT AND GET WHAT YOU LIKE, YOU'LL BE FORCED TO
LIKE WHAT YOU GET."

—GEORGE BERNARD SHAW

Lilian usually knows just what she wants and she never settles for
less than she deserves. Lilian's savv and strategic mind are constantly
saving her money. If push comes to shove, Lilian—always polite and
poised—shoves back, but she does it with such grace and finesse that
everyone involved in the genteel scuffle emerges without a scratch.

Lilian wanted to join a gym at the lowest possible cost. She did
some research and found the best deal in her neighborhood. Then
she rounded up two friends who were also interested, in order to approach the gym with a posse in tow. Because she was bringing in lots
of business in one fell swoop, she was able to negotiate a better rate
than she could have gotten as a single customer. She arranged the
deal on the phone, and agreed to meet the membership coordinator,
Dawn, at six that evening.

When Lilian and her merry band arrived, Dawn was not at the gym, but the manager, Andrew, a small man in a big suit who had been working at the gym only three nights, was. Lilian expressed her dismay at being stood up and the inconvenience of having to reschedule. When she intimated that she might take her business elsewhere, the novice manager snapped to attention. He promised to take care of everything right away. He darted off and quickly returned with the paperwork. Lilian decided to take the opportunity to sweeten the deal. She changed the payment schedule, the time frame, and negotiated extra guest passes and coupons for massages. Whenever Andrew looked like he might balk at her wishes, Lilian crinkled her nose and told him in the most pleasant terms that it simply wouldn't do. By the time the paperwork was completed, Lilian and company had a new gym, but Andrew had gotten the workout.

PRESENT CIRCUMSTANCES: GIFT GIVING

You may find it difficult to think about giving people anything but a run for their money—it is hard to feel generous when you've had to squelch your own material desires. Gift giving is a necessary act, but can be done sparingly. Think of it as yet another investment. You get as good as you give, as the old saying goes, so if you present your good friend with a bouquet of flowers and a fabulous home-cooked gourmet meal, you can expect similar graciousness in return. If you buy an exquisite pair of earrings for your confidante, you may receive that gorgeous silk scarf you've been ogling. Make a tape for your workmate, and he may return the favor with a gift certificate to your favorite CD emporium. If you find a year has passed since you have given a gift to a friend or family member, don't cry when your birthday and winter holiday season come without occasion.

Here are some nice gestures of mirth sharing, keeping minimal finances in mind:

- *Make it yourself.* Is there an artistic bone in your body, be it culinary, aural, or visual? Do you paint? Make good mix tapes? Cook a wicked chicken? If you are so gifted, make your own presents.
- *The joker is wild, and inexpensive.* Do you share inside jokes with your pals? Make them tangible. Go to your nearest novelty store to collect refrigerator magnets or rubber rodents. Check out the local flea market for an old movie poster, a vintage silver purse, a feather flapper hat, a used Twister game, or old election pins. Free your joke, and the frugality will follow.
- *The importance of being earnest.* If your friends are bookworms, or music addicts, and you are never sure if they own this book or that CD, take a chance and buy them something they couldn't possibly have. If they really do have everything, present them with a gift certificate to their favorite shop. It is their ticket to picking the gift of their choice.
- *Reach out and touch someone (or pay someone else to do it).* Is this friend tense in the shoulders, or in desperate need of pampering? Present her with a gift certificate for a massage, a manicure, a pedicure, or a facial. The thirty bucks you spend on your pal will make her feel like a million.
- *Tea for two, two for tea, and two years to pay up.* Are you seriously scrounging around for cash, but too embarrassed to see your birthday chum without a gift in hand? Offer to spend a one-on-one evening with the celebrator having drinks at a hotel bar, or treat him to a nice dinner . . . on your credit card. You will be entertained and fed, they will be appreciative, and you won't have spent a dime . . . yet.

That wasn't so painful, was it? The most you've spent here is thirty dollars, and some of these gifts directly benefit you. The satisfaction of a friend is worth the price of admission alone. When your own birthday arrives, throw yourself a party and count those chips.

Profile

Novelty Shopping

LARRY

When Larry gives a gift, he first senses where a friend's humor lies and then chooses something that appeals to that humor. He presented Brenda, his glambidextrous shopping companion, with an umbrella that, when closed, was shaped like a gigantic lipstick. Kate, his kitsch-loving co-worker, got her very own "Rappin' and Rockin'" Ken doll, complete with parachute pants, gold chain, and a battery-operated boom box. Eamon, the magnet collector, found himself the proud owner of a refrigerator magnet in the shape of, well, a refrigerator. Suzanne, the bouviessent girl in his friendship circle, was presented with Jackie O–like black sunglasses. Kathleen, the six-foot-tall gorgeous object of desire, who practically had to ask people to take a number, found a small bottle of some magical aphrodisiac and a gigantic hard rubber turtle awaiting her at her front door. And Larry's colleague Jason can now flush his quarters down his new toilet bank. These gifts may seem shameless, but Larry is always a satisfied gift giver: His recipients get a great laugh, and he never has to worry that they already have one of whatever he has doled out.

Profile

Make It Yourself: Gifts from the Hands of Those You [Will] Love

Christopher

What better gift than the soundtrack to your life? Christopher is the proud owner of a DAT machine (a high-quality tape deck with memory)—perfect for creating his yearly Christmas greeting tape to all of his friends and colleagues. Boasting a CD collection of more than fifteen hundred, not to mention a generous surplus of LPs and eight-track tapes, Christopher can put together a tape for any occasion, with music ranging from anything composed by Burt Bacharach (sung by favorites like Karen Carpenter and Dionne Warwick) to trip hop by Tricky, and an impressive selection of post-punkgrrrl bands. These musical treats are perfect for every occasion: birthdays, promotions, firings, Hanukkah, Kwanzaa, and Christmas. The artistry doesn't stop at the selection of tunes, either. Christopher custom designs the covers, with nifty images picked from his personal magazine collection, and typesets the song list on his PC. It costs him nothing but time, creativity, and a blank tape, and the happy recipients feel that they have been presented with a cartridge of gold.

David

David is a Renaissance man in every sense of the word. An actor, visual artist, writer, and comic, he oozes creativity from every pore. With gifts like these, why should he ever have to pay for presents? When he isn't making cutting comments in a stage whisper during business meetings, he can be found doodling intricate pears and fish. Because it seems a waste to restrict these beauties to a legal pad, David turns this talent to gift giving. For festivities where presents are protocol, he paints his elaborate fish and pears onto his collection of wooden cigar boxes, adding rhinestones, old photos, wire, and nails. The resulting objets d'art define exquisite. Every recipient of his boxes becomes a part of an elite group, and David remains a prince of a pauper.

Julia

It all began in the college dining hall over Rice Krispies dinners and heated political debates. Julia found herself twisting and shredding her napkins to keep her hands from throttling the neck of her irritating, impassioned dinner companion. These napkins began to take shape, metamorphosing into intricate dolls with petticoats, hats, angelic wings, and elaborate hands with long snaky fingers. Julia would carefully place them in her bag, and on fruitless Saturday nights, whip out the works in progress, and dab on some Elmer's glue to finish the crepe top or add fringe to the cape draping the paper shoulders. Soon, her frustration gave way to an immense collection of the most delicate and gorgeous paper-napkin dolls, which she gives as gifts to friends . . . and to make room for more.

Fruqal Finance

"I'M LIVING SO FAR BEYOND MY INCOME THAT WE MAY
ALMOST BE SAID TO BE LIVING APART."

—H. H. MUNRO

You don't have much money so you've got to do the best
you can given what you have to work with.

Enjoy Credit Cards

There's so much you can do with them: get free insurance
when you rent a car, establish a credit rating, earn frequent
flyer miles, buy things you can't afford, become engulfed
in a vicious gyre of spiraling debt, scrape paint off old furniture—the list goes on. Here are some thoughts on managing your credit cards.

More Is More.

Sign up for all of the credit cards you are offered for which
there are no annual fees, but don't keep more than one or
two Visas and MasterCards, unless you transfer your bal-
ances frequently (see next page). This includes department
store cards (which discount your first purchase and add
you to their mailing list) and gas cards. Consider signing
up for a card that awards frequent flyer miles with each
purchase (see Justin's Advice, page 183). Aim for gold
cards (which usually offer special services like rental car
insurance) and a corporate American Express card. Don't
ever miss a payment or default on a credit card. If you have
nothing else, you can at least have a good credit rating.
Note: You must be a really organized sort to pull this off.
If you are not a good filer, keep the cards to a minimum.

Can't Pay? Transfer.

Balance transfer is a buoy on the stormy sea of debt. If you have good credit and are on lots of mailing lists, as you should be (see Shopping, page 47), you are probably getting new credit card offers all the time. When you sign up for a new credit card, and at other random seasonal times, credit card companies invite you to transfer the balance of one card to another. (The company usually does this by sending a limited quantity of balance transfer checks, which you should hoard.) If you have a card with a balance you can't pay and a high interest rate, bounce the debt around each month from card to card, making sure to use the transfer checks, *not* the cash advance checks. This takes some attentive file management, but it may be worth it. If you have seven credit cards, you can comfortably absorb about ten thousand dollars' worth of debt without paying interest.

All You Had to Do Was Ask.

If you think your interest rate is high or you don't want to pay a fee (which you should *never* do except with a frequent flyer miles–earning card), call the customer service number on the back of your credit card and ask what their introductory interest rate is. If it is less than yours, say you'd like your rate lowered to that one. Companies usually comply without your having to deliver your "I've been a good customer for three years" routine. Same with fees: Call or write, say you've been fielding better offers, and ask them to waive the fee. Note: This also works with long-distance phone service. Call your company, say you hear a competitor has a better offer and ask what they can do for you. Then ask if the savings offer is retroactive. Play hardball.

PAY YOUR BILLS BEFORE YOU START TO SAVE

If you have a credit card whose annual percentage rate is 15 percent, and a small savings account whose interest rate is a horrendous 4 percent, you are a idiot if you don't pay the balance of the credit card before you start saving in the account. You will be losing money while fooling yourself into believing you are saving it.

PLAN AHEAD

Sign up for your 401K plan. Don't kid yourself. Social security is not going to be around when you retire, and you are not going to miss a few measly bucks each paycheck. It's worth it to plan ahead. The first place to save is in your 401K. When you have enough money to upgrade from Ramen to real semolina pasta, then consider other investments. Two words: compound interest.

SCRIMP

We do not suggest devoting Sunday mornings to clipping and filing coupons or going through the cushions of the couch in search of post-party favors. That's dowdy. Scrimping can be accomplished in much savvier—and more lucrative—ways:

Phone Sense.

Get call waiting and give priority to incoming long-distance calls. It doesn't matter with whom you were on the line first; whoever lives farthest away gets priority. C'est la vie! Your neighborhood buddies will get used to it.

Whenever possible, make personal calls from the office. Chatting with friends ("clients" if anyone asks) in distant climes is a pleasant and economical way to break up the work day.

Play tag. If you must return long-distance calls on your own nickel, do so when you know the person won't be in. Lunchtime is a safe bet.

Mail Sense.
What applies to phone calls applies to postage. Let the company pick up the tab. Look at it as a benefit comparable to health insurance. Tinker with mailing addresses slightly to make them look less suspicious: Send packages to your parents using your mother's maiden name (so the last name won't be the same as yours), make up phony businesses when you send mail to friends (for instance if you work in film, the address should read, "College Pal, The College Pal Talent Agency").

Don't Buy When You Can Rent.
Some books you want to own because you refer to them all the time. Others—novels you plan on reading only once—can be borrowed from the library. Roommates are for borrowing clothing and CDs. Movies can be seen on TV or during free cable weekends. Magazines can be read at the gym, some offices, and the hair salon.

Profile

OTHER PEOPLE'S MONEY

SHARON

Spending money feels good. It doesn't matter if it's not your own. Sharon discovered that spending other people's money makes for a satisfying spree every time.

Part of Sharon's job involves administering to the needs of fussy executives. They need flowers sent, cars ordered, gifts selected, and galas arranged. Sharon's boss slaps her corporate American Express card on Sharon's desk, tells her she trusts Sharon to handle things, and walks away. When she gets the green light, Sharon, an otherwise good-natured woman and freelance writer becomes a brassy, unyielding consumer, proving that power combined with good taste and a strong will is dangerous.

If Baccarat intimates that two specially engraved, gift-wrapped crystal vases may not be available for delivery today, Sharon threatens to call Steuben. The Baccarat vases arrive at their destination on time.

If Sharon gets the sense that Floralis might not understand that tiger lilies do not suit a hundred-dollar arrangement with an English garden–French chateau theme, she hints that Wine and Roses can do the job the way she wants it. The bouquet arrives as exquisite as Sharon had planned.

The seafood risotto costs more than the coq au vin? No matter. If Sharon feels it's worth it, the expense is added to her boss's bill and there's the end of it.

Her boss looks tired, is cranky, and Sharon would like to leave work early to go to the gym? Sharon takes the liberty of calling a car service to remove her boss from the office at once. Her boss is grateful for the suggestion, and Sharon sees her to her chariot and leaves work peacefully at five on the dot.

Money is meant to be spent, especially if it doesn't belong to you.

Profile

SEbAsTiAN

Sebastian went to the ATM one day to withdraw one hundred dollars when he noticed the promotion his bank was sponsoring. In order to encourage customers to use automated banking services, the ATMs were programmed to award eighty dollars at random times to people withdrawing money. Instead of withdrawing the one hundred dollars he needed in a lump sum, Sebastian withdrew five hundred dollars in twenty-dollar increments. (Five hundred dollars is the maximum withdrawal a customer can make in one twenty-four-hour period; twenty dollars is the minimum withdrawal amount.) By increasing the number of times he used the ATM, he increased his odds of winning the eighty-dollar prize money. But he didn't win. So he deposited four hundred and eighty dollars and took twenty home with him.

The next day he returned to the ATM and repeated the process, this time withdrawing four hundred and eighty dollars and depositing four hundred and sixty dollars. He returned every day to the bank and tried to win the prize until the promotion ended several weeks later.

Sebastian never hit the jackpot but at least he was a contender. His diligence in playing the bank's ATM like a free slot machine is to be commended. When you have a shot at the brass ring, grab it.

You Can't Always Get What You Want, But If You Try Sometime, You Just Might Find, You Dominate

Mick—the other Jagger—had it right. (We are paraphrasing his immortal observation.) Sometimes people will try to block your will. Don't let them. You have the upper hand; you know what you want, and you have the poise and confidence to get it. Follow this advice and you will prevail in nearly every conflict.

- *Quietly insist.* Assume that you will get your way and that there has been a misunderstanding. Don't raise your voice; rather, explain pleasantly why you are right and the other person is wrong. Sometimes the person will give in right away.
- *Ask to speak to the manager.* You must be speaking to a person of relative power in order to get things done. If the person to whom you are speaking isn't budging, chances are he or she can't change things. Managers usually can. Don't ask for the manager as a bluff or you may be called on it.
- *Turn up the volume.* In some cases, at the threat of a scene, people will relent and let you have your way. They don't want other customers to be upset by a disturbance.

This is especially true at airports (see Profile: Aisha at the Airport, page 192).

▪ *Make a scene.* When you were a child, a "scene" was known as a "temper tantrum." The marks of a scene include broad gestures, shouting, crying, and dragging other people into the fray. Use scenes sparingly. They are exhausting and ugly (try not to make one in front of a lover). They are often effective, however, so gauge the situation. If you think a scene will work and feel it must be done, give it a go.

▪ *Write a letter; cc everyone.* If you got rotten service on a flight, were promised a massage at a gym but were later denied it, or were mistreated in any way, consider writing a letter to remedy things. Letter writing gives you time to collect your thoughts away from the hysteria of the crisis and indicates a heightened level of concern. Anyone can shout at a service desk; few people do the work of finding out to whom a letter ought to go and sitting down to write one. Those who do are usually compensated—with an apology if nothing else.

Write the names of the people you are sending copies to on the bottom of the letter so that your grievance is made more public and embarrassing for the offending party. Include the appropriate governmental agency, local media, and/or friends who are lawyers. For example, if you were badly treated on an airplane, you should let the airline know that you are alerting the F.A.A., as well as national and local travel writers, to the shoddy service you were given.

Entertainment

Champagne in a Can, Caviar in Your Dreams

"NOTHING SUCCEEDS LIKE EXCESS."

—OSCAR WILDE

Entertaining yourself in high style on a low income sounds dreary. Perk up, Sunshine. Swank is within your grasp. In fact, the pursuit of economical entertainment is half the fun. It takes the creativity of an artist, the chutzpah of a used-car salesman, and the pretense of a thespian—all of which you should possess. Sure, anyone can buy fun with unlimited funds, but few can party on a pittance. Join the few and the proud, and watch your life get exciting.

In this chapter, we survey your entertainment venues. Like high school sporting events, cheap thrills can be broken up into two categories: home and away. Staying at home (or at the home of someone else) is the easiest way to save money. Food, drinks, and movies intended for home consumption are all cheaper than their out-on-the-town counterparts. But home thrills usually take more work (planning, cleaning, culinary preparation), and though home activity is often rewarding, there are times when you need to let the city streets control your destiny for a night.

When you don't have it in you to be the host[ess] with the most[est], you've got to take your show on the road. The one drawback: It is easy to blow your tiny cash wad in one extravagant pop. Read on and learn how to paint the town red while remaining in the black.

THE ENTERTAINMENT QUIZ

1 A close friend invites you to a first-tier restaurant, and you've just paid rent, with one hundred dollars left to get you through to the next paycheck. How do you handle the situation without admitting financial duress?

a. Put the dinner on your credit card and have your friend give you cash for his share.

b. Say you had a large lunch earlier, and suggest coffee and dessert, as you'd love to see the friend tonight.

c. Invite your diner over for dinner, and to his question of what to bring, answer, "a nice big bottle of wine."

d. Have a peanut butter and jelly sandwich at home, and then order a bowl of the ribollita at the restaurant.

e. Break down and confess your duress, and hope that he offers to treat, or is willing to eat pizza.

2 You've trumpeted party plans for Saturday to friends, promising to follow up with details. Your tax return returns with some sobering news: They don't owe you money; rather you owe them—big time. How do you subsidize your fete?

a. Change it from crème brulée and canapes to a white trash theme party and ask your friends to bring Jell-O shots, bourbon, and/or Old Style beer in a can. Prepare pigs-in-blankets, Tater Tots, and vinegar pie for your guests.

b. Move the party to a sparsely attended bar and do a takeover.

c. Host an early cocktail party instead of a knock-down-drag-out.

d. You don't. You cancel.

e. Take charge of your life with your Visa, and forge ahead with your original plan.

3 It's Thursday, the weekend looms. You have thirty-four dollars you can use to entertain yourself. How do you allocate the funds?

a. Friday: Go for drinks with work friends, go home, get takeout, go to bed by eleven. Value: ten dollars; Saturday: Go to a swanky hotel bar, the Four Seasons, for example, with three feisty friends. Order a round of Cosmopolitans. Loiter with the shakers (which contain two and a half actual drinks) then move to the bargain cinema. Your share: fourteen dollars; Sunday: Have brunch, consider and decide against going into the office, read the paper, relax, call friends to report on your weekend. Value: ten dollars.

b. Friday: Go for drinks with work friends and eat enough free finger foods at the bar to call it dinner; meet other friends for dessert and coffee, go to their house with a movie rental. Value: twelve dollars; Saturday: Throw an impromptu party with your roommates. When invitees ask what they can bring, say beer or wine. Value: twelve dollars; Sunday: Have brunch, consider and decide against going into the office, read the paper, relax, call friends to report on your weekend. Value: ten dollars.

c. Friday: Blow a wad of wallet on cover and drinks at a music lounge to see that band that intrigues you so. Take a cab home. Value: twenty-four dollars; Saturday: Call and tell that friend with the wet dream deferred that you are ready to cash in your sex rain check in exchange for a nice bottle of merlot, some latex, and a promise of discretion. Value: zero dollars; Sunday: Have brunch, consider and decide against going into the office, read the paper, relax, call friends to report on your weekend. Value: ten dollars.

d. Friday: Culinary artists Sharon and David have invited you and a friend for an elegant dinner party, and have insisted you bring nothing. You bring flowers, your date, and some sorbet. Your share of the total cost: six dollars; Saturday: Go to a poetry slam at a downtown cafe, have dinner at an inexpensive Indian restaurant, swing by a big bash with a six-pack of Rolling Rock, drink Scotch, do a shot of tequila with strangers, make a sweep of the apartment and realize the friend who'd invited you never showed, take a cab home. Value: eighteen dollars; Sunday: Have brunch, consider and decide against going into the office, read the paper, relax, call friends to report on your weekend. Value: ten dollars.

4   It is 10:30 on a Saturday night. You've had a few drinks, but aren't yet buzzed. The party is starting to wane, and you are ready for plan *B*. Several drug situations present themselves to you, and you are easily seduced, especially since you've enjoyed each of these drugs in moderation in the past. You must keep in mind that your boss returns from vacation on Monday, so you have to be coherent, punctual, and lucid in thirty-six hours; use this to inform your decision. You can:

a. Follow half of the party to your old roommate's apartment to do bong hits.

b. Go to a close friend's place and snort her last two dime bags of heroin with her.

c. Do coke all night with your friend from work.

d. Drop a hit of Ecstasy with someone you've just met at the dwindling party.

e. Go home, smoke a joint, and go to bed.

5 The singles scene has grown tiresome for you. You decide to shoot for commitment. These are your options. Rate the best (1 being most favorable):

a. A great lay with no job.

b. An innocuous investment banker.

c. A close friend with whom you share sexual tension.

d. A philandering music executive.

e. A hip, shy doctoral candidate on fellowship.

ANSWERS:

1. If you've chosen **b**, give yourself four points. Your goal should always be to downgrade the event to something less burdensome than dinner. Coffee and dessert make sense. You get to see your friend, go out for atmosphere, and you don't have to worry about overspending. No one will know you ate Ramen alone. **D** is the next logical option—three points. You go to the restaurant, but order the least expensive thing there. No chance you'll be expected to pay more than your share. **C** forces you to admit you are broke and demands your labor, but makes for a cozy evening a deux. **A** is tempting, but not a good idea. You'll feel the meal coming up again when you get your scary credit card bill. Exception: If you are expenseploiting the meal it's okay to charge it (*not* okay to ask your friend for money in that case); if your credit

card is linked to a frequent flyer account, this is alright but remember, you still have to pay next month. **E** is a sniveling excuse
not to indulge. Never admit defeat in this way. Find a way to have
your cake and eat it too.

2. **A** flaunts your creativity and the kids love the kitsch of a theme
party. They haven't done Jell-O shots since college. Give yourself
four points. If you chose **e**, your courage is to be commended.
While you can avoid going to a restaurant, you can't duck out of
something happening at your place. Charge ahead and hope there
are leftovers you can live off for the next week. Three points.
While **b** alleviates your stress of setup and cleanup, it transfers
the burden to your friends' wallets. Two points. If you picked **c**,
wrong! A cocktail party is more expensive than a knock-down-
drag-out. It's earlier, so people expect some good food and perhaps mixed drinks. At a knock-down-and-drag-out you don't
need much more than a lot of beer and good music to keep your
pals hopping. One point. You get no points for **d**. Canceling is the
act of a coward. And we don't mean Noël.

3. With **b**, a nice monetary balance is struck between Friday and
Saturday. After a tiring workweek, you want something mellow
for Friday. Saturday you've slept in and have time to throw together a little party. **C** also means a fun time, but you've spent almost everything on Friday, leaving slim pickings for Saturday.
You are taking a risk on Saturday. What if she's not there? What
if he's not as good as you've heard? What if she's found another?
Unless gambling excites you as much as sex, there are too many
variables here. If you chose **d**, the Friday dinner is fabulous, but
Saturday is a wash. You didn't get your act together and plans
were foiled. The potential was there but it wasn't meant to
be. And you ended up buying beer for a party you spent five min-

utes at. If you chose **a**, *Hello!* a place like Four Seasons is a mid-week, after-work treat. You don't go there on a Saturday. Zero points.

4. Bong hits (**a**) are the logical choice if you are facing a high-stress Monday. Smoking the wacky won't knock you down for too long. After a night of pot, you sleep well with no side effects. If the party is already waning (**e**), maybe you should call it a night. Smoke a cozy joint alone at home and get a good night's sleep. Two dime bags of heroin (**b**) is not enough to put you out for the whole weekend, but it's more intense than pot. Sunday will be a waste, and while you're on the stuff, your skin will itch. If you start doing coke now (**c**), you are going to feel like hell and be in pain Monday morning. This is no way to start the workweek. Ecstasy (**d**) takes a real toll on your body; you won't have recovered by Monday. Also, never do it with strangers. Maybe with a friend on a Friday, but not a Saturday.

5. A university fellow (**e**) will be home to do housework, and love you without relying upon your finances. Granted, fellows can't always take you to dinner, but they usually have the time and interest to make you dinner. A banker (**b**) will never make you pay. He's not the stuff of romantic fantasies, but he's nice and game to do things when he's free. Reliability and decadence look smart even in a pinstripe wrapper. The great lay (**a**) is not going to give you goods, but he'll give you good loving. You may be pulling the purse strings, but that's a small price to pay for good sex. Close pals (**c**) are not preferred; the great things about his friendship may grate when you become lovers. If he's absolutely not exfriendable, don't do it. If you chose **d**, remember: while the perks of free concerts and CDs and meeting your music idols are seductive, it's commitment you're after. Don't go there.

ON THE TOWN: LEISURE PURSUITS

Cultured Pearls of Wisdom

"I MAY DIE BEFORE A TRAIN OF THOUGHT ENTERS THE STATION."

—DOROTHY PARKER

In order to know how to live, you must live in the know. There's no better whetstone on which to hone kaffeeklatsch and cocktail conversation skills than reading material. The daily newspaper is the most important source of information. Read it at least six times a week (if you need a day of rest, skip the Saturday edition). Absorb the Arts & Leisure section, op-ed page, and the obituaries. Browse through major metro, national, and international news, and glance at the business section. This is your skeleton of knowledge, but without the skin and the meat, you are not yet there. Flesh it out with doses of the supplements that follow. When you synthesize all of this information, you'll have assembled a witty, informed banter ready to wear for any social occasion.

You don't need to see every art show, attend every film screening, eat at every hot restaurant, nor read every book in order to have seemingly informed insights. You can't possibly spend 90 percent of your free time, and all that money—you just don't have it. Voracious reading enables you to live vicariously.

Infauxmation—borrowed knowledge, the ultimate act of appropriation—is your shortcut to good banter. Arm yourself during train rides, Sunday mornings, canceled lunch dates, with the widest variety of reading material. Find critics you love and trust; critics you hate; listen in on conversations at work and at play, and consider these resources the Cliff's Notes to cultured life. Here is a list of required reading, followed by recommended reading. Remember, half of glambidextrosity is being infauxmed, and eighty percent of being a Frugal Indulgent means being glambidextrous. Heed our call, and read on:

REQUIRED READING

a quality daily newspaper (*The New York Times, Boston Globe, Los Angeles Times, Washington Post, Baltimore Sun*, etc.)

a mainstream media mag (*Entertainment Weekly* or *People*)

a women's fashion rag (*Vogue* and *Harper's Bazaar*)

a hot feature compendium (*The New Yorker* or *Vanity Fair*)

a music magazine (*Spin, Vibe,* or *Rolling Stone*)

a women's feature magazine (*Elle, Allure,* or *Glamour*)

a political/arts analysis rag (*Harper's, The Nation, The New Republic, The Utne Reader,* or *The Atlantic Monthly*)

a men's monthly fashion/feature publication (*Details, Esquire,* or *GQ*)

your metropolitan-area monthly magazine (*Boston Magazine, Paper* [NYC], *Texas Monthly, New York, TimeOut, Chicago Magazine*)

an alternative city paper (*The Village Voice, The Chicago Reader, The Boston Phoenix*)

WE ALSO RECOMMEND

The Wall Street Journal

your city's free weekly paper

an entertainment industry magazine (*Movieline, Buzz,* or *Premiere*)

the city book review

a men's entertainment mag (*Playboy* or *Penthouse*—the articles really are great, and the photos are a kick—boobs don't really look like *that*)

a trade magazine of your field (*Hollywood Reporter, ArtForum, Publishers Weekly, Variety, Adweek, Billboard, Backstage, Financial Times*)

a culinary magazine (*Gourmet, Bon Appetit, Cook's Magazine*, or *Food & Wine*)

a dream house publication (*Martha Stewart Living, House & Garden, Metropolitan Home*, or *Architectural Digest*)

a gay/lesbian mag (*The Advocate, Out, Genre*, or *Girlfriends*, or *Deneuve*)

a teen rag (*Seventeen, YM*, or *Sassy;* find out what the kids are up to)

You might not like every publication you read, but it is important to be as informed as possible, whether it's being up on the latest heroin-related death of a favorite rock star or the leftist perspective of the strife in Bosnia. When these issues arise in conversation, you'll be prepared.

I LIKE THE NIGHTLIFE, I LOVE TO BOOGIE: GOING OUT

The benefit of city living is, of course, its endless diversions for a wide range of pockets. There are restaurants to dine in, bars to wine in, films and theater to see, people to do. The trick is getting the most for the least.

Eating Out

Restaurant going transforms one of life's necessities into a jaunt. It is fun. It is social. But, don't kid yourself: It is recklessly decadent. Restaurant food is infinitely more expensive than a home-cooked meal. If you are hot to save money, this is a logical place to slash your budget. (As shrewd spender Saylor Breckenridge once observed: A human being can easily survive for at least a week on nothing but peanut butter and jelly sandwiches.) Yes, this raises quality-of-life issues. But it boils down to priorities. If food is important to you and you are determined to eat it outside of your apartment, consider some tips that will save you a few dollars!

EXPENSEPLOITATE IT. Charge dinner to your expense account. Wake up: If you have an expense account and are not using it to combine business with pleasure, you are not making the most of your benefits package.

You and a friend are having dinner. Why not take that fun client along, talk business for a few minutes, and call it work?

Are your friends even peripherally involved in your industry? Then they are not just friends, they are contacts and colleagues. Treat them as such, and treat them—and yourself—to a nice dinner.

Have a friend with an expense account buy you dinner. This is why it is important to have some older friends more advanced in their careers. They find buoyant youth at the dinner table refreshing and will pay to be entertained by it.

MAKE IT COFFEE AND DESSERT. MAKE IT DRINKS. MAKE IT BRUNCH. Dinner is the most expensive meal of the day, so for God's sake, unless someone else is picking up the check— be it a corporation (see Expenseploitation, above) or an individual (see Date, below), avoid it. Unless it is a dive, a charming ethnic restaurant, or a rare splurge, try to turn dinner into something less expensive. Keep in mind that even ordering cheap items at an inexpensive restaurant may not work to save you money if, at the end of the evening, the check is split evenly among you (house salad) and the others (lobster).

Coffee and Dessert. This works well when you have after-dinner plans with a group. Offer regrets and say you'll catch up with them at meal's end. Try these excuses: "Already ate, had a late lunch, feel mildly queasy, working late."

Drinks. Here's a chance to try a new spot, ideally one that has free nibblies, or barring that, a spectacular view. Consider ordering a thick stout beer, most of which have a consistency only slightly thinner than bread, and drink your dinner for a fraction of the cost.

Brunch. If you can move the date from night to day, do. Brunch is the most cost-effective meal of the day. You can coast on that one meal—consumed midday—until breakfast the next day. There are affordable brunch specials all over town, loitering is often tolerated or encouraged, and brunch consolidates two meals into one.

DATE. Granted, it remains easier for a woman to go on a date with a man and hope he'll pay, but the reverse is not impossible. As far as gay protocol is concerned: Don't ask, don't pay. In other words, if you didn't ask the person out, you can't possibly be expected to foot the entire tab. At the very least, Dutch will be the egalitarian arrangement, but more often than not, the invitor will not expect the invitee to contribute a dime. If a second date follows, the invitee and the invitor can switch roles, and you can expect to reciprocate.

The guilt of not paying for your fair share on a date can be dissipated easily by dating (1) people who are older and more firmly established in their careers, (2) people with trust funds, (3) lawyers, bankers, and other fiscally advantaged careerists, and (4) boring people who deserve to pay for your having endured the tedium of their presence.

GO TO DIVES. Everything in moderation, especially slumming it. But sometimes you've got to do it. Go for cheap Chinese food and enjoy the bad but complimentary (though it *complements* none of the food) chardonnay. Have scrambled eggs, home fries, and coffee for dinner at the local greasy spoon. Go to a fringe neighborhood to eat authentic, delicious food while you soak up the trippy decor for a few dollars.

EAT LESS AT BETTER PLACES. It's often better to get less of a good thing than more of a crummy one. (This applies to clothes and sex as well as food, but rarely to apartment space.) Go to the bar at the best place in town and have a big appetizer or salad for dinner. New York City's Gramercy Tavern, for instance, is an excellent place to do this. It is an expensive restaurant with a limited menu and a great beer list for people who drink at the bar. You'll get three-star ambience, and the food (and the portions, regrettably) will be a fraction of the cost. Caution: This is best done with one other conspirator who is also an effective glamour scrimper, not with unwieldy groups, in which spending can spiral out of control.

CHECK INTO HOTEL BARS. The bars in some hotels offer unlimited free hot hors d'oeuvres with their drinks. The schmaltzy atmosphere of these fading belles (you're unlikely to get something for nothing in a chichi place, so pick your hotel by the cheesy lobby carpeting) and the free chicken wings, pretzel and nut mixes, dumplings, and tortilla chips make them worthy "dinner" stops.

CHARGE IT. It feels like you're making a profit when you charge a meal: You don't pay a dime on site and your fellow diners give you their shares in cash. This is an attractive, albeit misleading and dangerous way to eat well as you rack up frequent flyer miles on your mile-earning credit card (see A Few Words on Frequent Flying, page 183).

GRAZE. Rather than eating a formal lunch at a real restaurant, go to your local specialty foods shop. There, amid the smoked meats and foreign cheeses, you'll find free sample platters designed to get you to buy large quantities of those items. Pick up a toothpick and have a taste or two or three. (It may take you several bites to determine that you don't want to buy the prosciutto.) Move on to the next counter and repeat. Soon, you'll be so stuffed you won't be able to look at another toothpick.

Another great pasture for grazing is catered parties. Art openings, book signings, and auction previews usually offer nibblies that circulate on trays. Determine where the kitchen is, then post yourself by the door to ensure that you are in the line of fire as the caterers haul out the goodies.

BREAD ALONE. This tactic is reserved for the shameless and truly desperate. Go to a not-so-busy, decent restaurant. When the maitre d' invites you in, say that you are expecting a friend but will wait at the table. The waiters will then bring you bread (maybe a nice focaccia) and water (if they ask, "Minerale?" you respond, "No, thanks. Municipale."). Slowly eat the whole bread basket, occasionally looking at the door and your watch. When you finish the last crumb, pack up, and apologize to the maitre d'. You can't possibly fathom where your date could be. You hope he's alright. Make your graceful, if contrite, exit.

Sights and Sounds

If you don't consume food when you are out on the town, you can stuff yourself on culture without becoming poor or fat.

MUSEUMS. They aren't just for tourists anymore. Museums offer fun and inspiration with no opportunity to buy things (save for items in the cute gift shop, which you should avoid at all costs). Lots of museums are virtually free, including the Smithsonian Museums and New York's Metropolitan Museum of Art. Those that charge admission usually set aside one free day (usually a weekday evening). If a museum is not free, and you can't miss that retrospective, use your college I.D. for a reduced student pass. That I.D. typically works for several years after graduation. (Who looks closely at anything but the embarrassing photo?)

Auction houses have previews of their collections that are open to the public at no charge. There you'll see offbeat tchotchkes and masterpieces traveling between private collections that may never make it to your local museum. The art at auction houses is for sale (and pieces are marked with estimates), but not at tempting prices.

CONCERTS. Here you are offered a panoply of interesting options. Concerts in parks, concerts in museums, concerts by struggling bands in smoky basement bars, concerts in tiny jazz bistros, Broadway showcases. These sorts of events are inexpensive, and in some cases, free, so they are the ones you ought to attend. Avoid stadium shows—that was high school fare. You've outgrown the disappointment of a crowded rip-off; it's time to attend those intimate gems.

If you are interested in what are perhaps the most expensive types of concerts—operas, classical music recitals, etc.—and don't want to pay top dollar try these tactics:

- *Speak up.* Let your older colleagues know that you are an oboe/opera/ballet enthusiast. Few people your age are, and even fewer are vocal about it. If someone has a theater subscription and can't attend (which happens more frequently than you might think), you may benefit. Culture buffs don't like wasting expensive tickets and get a kick out of a young person's interest in more mature pursuits.
- *Take a chance on it.* Risk swinging by the theater one half hour before curtain to see if there are people outside trying to unload extra tickets. The price they'll accept for them declines as showtime looms, so hold out for a deal. Police tend to look away from the misdemeanors of well-attired patrons of large civic arts complexes, so the chances of your being busted in a scalping operation are low.
- *Go when the weather is bad.* Many theatergoers are from affluent suburbs surrounding cities, and when the weather is inclement they don't risk driving in. Go to the box office of a sold-out show and buy a standing room ticket. Go to your assigned post, scope out the house, and five minutes before the curtain rises, take the velvety seat of your choice.

- *Investigate youth subscriptions.* These are to boost membership and encourage patronage in years to come (get 'em hooked while they're young). Many subscription packages are reasonable, and they are certainly an elegant splurge.
- *Tiptoe through the two doors.* New York City's *Paper* magazine recommended this strategy for fanatics who will take whatever they can get: Arrive at the theater at intermission with an old issue of *Playbill* rolled up so the cover is hidden. Blend in with the legitimate patrons when they come out for fresh air, then file back in with them and take a seat in the balcony or stand in the back. You'll see only half the show, but the price is right.

BOOKSTORES. Bookstores these days encourage shameless browsing and let you read in peace. They are becoming pickup scenes as well, especially at the magazine racks, and they are a better place than bars to find suitable dates because you can stalk your quarry by interest. If you do decide to join the hunt, keep in mind the following:

- *Do not overlook the science fiction and computers sections.* All that D&D playing and extracurricular programming has resulted in high-paying technology jobs and a lingering shyness. Reach out to a grown-up nerd and you may be rewarded with a nice suitor who can actually pay for a nice dinner.
- *Check out the magazine section if there is one.* It's a mingling mecca.
- *Avoid certain sections like Self-Help and New Age/Spirituality.* These are red flags for trouble.
- *Don't sit.* Bookstores feature lots of seats these days. Avoid them. When you are looking for action, you must stay on your toes.

MOVIES. Movies have become what theater used to be: an expensive indulgence, but it is still possible to find some good deals.

- *Go to retrospectives at museums.* Many museums, libraries, and cultural societies screen films for affordable sums. If the movie is at a museum, go on a free night or invite a member with you.
- *Get free passes.* In some cities stores give away screening passes to new movies. Tickets are given away on a first come, first serve basis, so if you read the newspaper like a good early bird (see Cultured Pearls of Wisdom, page 100) and see the ad right away, you'll get your share of free worms. In major cities, you can attend test screenings of movies that are still being edited. You have to endure a quiz at the end, but for denizens of these movie towns, it's worth it to feel in the know.
- *Make it a double feature.* If you can't halve the price, you ought to double the volume.
- *Wait for the three-dollar theater.* Many cities have second-run theaters, so if you can wait to see it, do.
- *Go to a matinee.* Most cities offer matinees. Although it may be slightly less exciting to see some shows in the afternoon, it is considerably less expensive.
- *Avoid the multiplex.* If you've got to see the new Robert Altman in the first week of release (and pay top dollar), at least see it in a fabulous theater. See it in an art deco boutique or a grand, balconied independent or someplace with spacious seats and good coffee. Make the splurge worth it.

BARS

When there's nothing else to do, there's always drinking. Liquor is a wonderful thing. It makes shy people outgoing, boring dates fun;

it increases longevity (according to the latest research); and it tastes good too. The only downside: It tends to be expensive. Next time you have the urge to tie one on, try this advice:

- *Go to happy hour.* Hitting a good happy hour involves a little preliminary research to find out which bar has the best deals for drinking at off-peak times. Doing the field research, in this case, is half the fun.
- *Find a value-added bar.* If you are going to pay full price for drinks, find a bar that boasts some amenities. Are nibblies offered? Is there live music? A breathtaking view from a rotating cutout in the floor? Kitschy decor? Make sure you get what you pay for.
- *Become a regular.* If you go to a place where everybody knows your name and is always glad you came, you'll get preferred customer status in the form of discounted if not complimentary drinks.
- *Swank in moderation/Dive in headfirst.* If you are just going to have one drink, go to someplace swanky. The bar at the Four Seasons offers Cosmopolitans (which are so full of booze, one drink feels like three) for eleven dollars. For Four Seasons atmosphere and generous portions, you are getting a bargain. If you plan on making a night of it, go to a dive where you can buy five-dollar pitchers, get cheap shots with beer, etc.
- *Avoid bars that advertise "women drink free."* The warning is spelled out right there in the window. You'll be asking for fraternity basement decor and trouble. (Remember *The Accused?*)

LOUNGE, DON'T CLUB

The quickest way to throw money down the drain is to go clubbing. Why should you have to pay fifteen to twenty dollars to go to a sterile open space with bad techno music and hundreds of quasmopolitans dressed as Londoners of five to ten years past? Seems tired, eh? The drinks are expensive—six dollars for a small plastic cup of Budweiser, and the ecstasy the kids are selling for ten dollars is usually just No Doz. There is no fun to be had, only disappointment.

Clubbing is eighties fare, anyway, and if you recall, the eighties were known for Reagan, Bush, yuppies, legwarmers and the *Flashdance* look, eating blowfish, and snorting immense amounts of cocaine. Some of the coolest people died during the eighties—Andy Warhol, Jean-Michel Basquiat, John Lennon, Halston, Keith Haring, to name a few. They missed out on little, clubwise, except for the emergence of the best mediocre new wave music around.

Lounging is the clubbing of the 1990s. You sit on couches, drink beer, and for a small cover charge, see some groovy bands, be they country, rock and roll, or acid jazz. The ambience is far more intimate and entertaining, and the kids don't try to clone themselves as much. Lounges are far more conducive to meeting people with common interests (or meeting people, period). Overall, a much more satisfying experience, sans pretention.

Here are some suggestions to consider:

- *Go to bars with excellent jukeboxes.* For loose change you can arrange the soundtrack to your evening and bond with fellow bargoers over songs you haven't heard since junior high.
- *Go to small bars with a DJ.* These are still cheap (there's rarely a cover charge) and full of ambience, and people may move the chairs and infect the place with dance fever.
- *Go to bars with pool tables.* You'll meet some people and pay half of what you would at a pool hall.
- *Go to gay/lesbian bars.* Off nights at these places offer a casual, fun-loving, local scene. Fridays and Saturdays often attract quasmopolitans, but it's good for slutrocious encounters.

Profile

Two Cents' Worth

Anna

As a freelance writer/editor living in a small studio apartment, Anna finds that entertaining more than one guest at a time and working at home proves difficult. The local coffee emporium, however, provides ample space for her portable office, as well as for meeting friends for caffeination. At this particular hangout, Anna holds court for seven hours at a time on one double espresso. She can be found on any given day at the big round table near the back, with laptop perched in front of her, paper cup filled with congealing milk to her left, backpack stuffed with the day's necessities to her right, and three paperbacks sprawled on the table. Sometimes she can be found pounding away on the keyboard, with the remaining chairs empty, while other times, she is seen taking friendly appointments throughout the day, as people arrive in shifts. Whole manuscripts have been edited, articles for national magazines written, and social updates given at this table. The best part? The price to maintain the office space/living room comes to $2.50 a day, and the café staff has no intention of imposing time limits.

Linda

Linda has been partially employed for well over a year, but has acted as a full-time friend to many for the greater part of her adult life. While she finds that it is difficult to keep up with everyone—as it costs a bundle to go out—she will not let a measly financial problem squelch her outings. It takes compromise, but Linda embraces it with both arms and six dollars. Not a drink guzzler, but a woman who appreciates a stiff drink in small doses, Linda can make a dry vodka martini (with three olives) last no less than an hour and a half. Eager to experience the new hot restaurants, bars, and grills, but aware that six dollars will not even get her a bowl of soup, she approaches this conflict with a winning solution: She meets her friends at the restaurants' bars, and makes an evening out of one drink. She can always offer a critique about the clientele, the staff, and the martinis—a shortcut in evaluating the restaurant's quality. One does not need to know if the food at Trattoria Qualcosa di Bello or Chez Quelqu'un is brilliant—you can read about *that* in the city magazines. One can assume that the food is, in fact, delicious. But, clientele is to be experienced firsthand, and with a martini in the other hand, even a pauper with one good outfit can size up the situation for herself.

Jeremy

Open the bar and Jeremy is there, be it a new club in town or an office Christmas party. At a bar and grill for a book party, or at the local lounge for a promotional record party, you can find Jeremy with two beers in one hand, a glass of wine and a screwdriver in the other. Sometimes he shares them with an accompanying friend, but more often than not, you will find him at a table in the back with literally three drinks under the table, and one in hand. Most open bars have a time limit, so Jeremy hoards accordingly, though discreetly. In doing so, Jeremy can cruise for weeks at a time, being entertained on the corporate dime—mind you, not that of his own company. He is not expenseploitating. If it was drinks he was after, he could always get someone to buy him one. Hell, he could even buy his own. But Jeremy gets enjoyment from open bars the way others flock to an all-you-can-eat special at the local smorgasbord. He tips the bartenders generously—so as not to seem cheap—is generous in offering drinks to others, and always comes off as the king of the party. He visits clubs he would ordinarily never enter, attends parties for books and music he would never buy, and bonds with strangers he doesn't work with. Jeremy will take in the scenery of any world offering him free bar time, and in doing so he collects an eclectic group of friends and interests, along with the inevitable surplus of hangovers. But, because most open bars end early, he uses the time limit to his advantage, taking the cue to call it a night by 9:00 P.M., appearing fresh and lucid by morning, refreshed enough to do it all over again the next day.

TEN BUCKS BOX

As a general Frugal Indulgents' rule, all a person under thirty really needs to entertain herself in a major metropolitan area is ten bucks and a credit card, neither of which will necessarily be used by evening's end. These are props to procure fun and frolic—once you settle into a social situation, the likelihood of having to spend a dime lessens, and your net worth increases as your older pals load you up with free outings and opportunities. Entertaining yourself rarely calls for committing Salvation Armani—save that for your wear, your rent, your vacation.

Let's take the ten-buck rule as literally as possible. Assume this hypothetical situation: If you were to really be obligated to spend ten dollars, how far would it take you?

- dinner at a diner for one
- three joints
- two beers with tip at a bar, or four beers with a cheap tip during happy hour
- a cab ride home
- parking a car in a lot for two hours
- a movie for one with small soda
- a ticket to a regional theatrical production, maybe
- a pack of cigarettes, a pack of gum, the Sunday paper, and a six-pack of Bud in cans
- three to four movie rentals
- two bottles of Carlo Rossi Paisano, a light Chianti
- pasta noodles (ziti, fusilli, linguini, take your pick), canned tomatoes, a head of garlic, fresh basil, and a small block of parmesan cheese
- twenty pounds of washed, dried, and folded laundry
- three newsstand magazines or two porn mags

You get the general idea. The less prudent the concept, the more bang for your buck[s]. If you are invited out for dinner by the older, wiser, and more gainfully employed folk, your response should be as follows: "I'd love to join you, but I'm a bit short on cash." The guaranteed response: "We'll prorate and/or cover you, because we haven't seen you in so long." Scarcity makes your presence more valuable, and chances are, your value will give way to paid dinners, movies, drugs, whatever your heart desires. Make sure to distribute your appreciated presences and absences evenly, always make the effort to pay (so you don't seem like a freeloader), and you'll find yourself coasting weeks at a time on the same ten bucks, while the Visa card remains virginal.

All Messed Up and No Place to Go: Drugs

"SPEED PROVIDES THE ONE GENUINELY MODERN PLEASURE."

—ALDOUS HUXLEY

It is 1:30 A.M., and the party is wrapping up. You may be a bit drunk, but not trashed; a bit cloudy, but not messed up. You are definitely not ready for bed; you *are* ready for more substances.

You've just been through an excruciating week, and you feel you've earned the right to DWI, drink or drug while intoxicated. The host is yawning excessively, and you're not hazy enough to be oblivious to the hint. You go to the coat room (previously a bedroom), find your coat with ease (there are only three left on the futon), and find a few other wired folks to join you on the escapade you will regret by Monday.

While your inner child may be acting out, your outer adult should be slightly calculating, if not pragmatic. Remember, you may love good frivolous fun, but you still have grown-up responsibilities, like that job you're trying to hold down.

Mull over these suggestions before you indulge:

- *Drugs require time and money.* These are two things you can't afford to waste. Let your situation be guided by your obligations. If you have an early morning meeting on Monday, and a close friend invites you to snort dope on a Friday evening, go crazy. You have Saturday to sleep, and Sunday to catch up with yourself. But if you plan to indulge in drug fun on a Saturday night at 11:00

P.M., stick with pot—Sunday isn't enough recovery time for the demands of coke, ecstasy, acid, heroin, and their friends.

- *Don't ever pay for drugs.* Ingratiate yourself with those who do. Hang out with recreational users. They love the company, the adventure, the possibilities. Someone always has a joint that needs sharing. If your drug tastes are decadent, mooch a hit of ecstasy off a dealer who is peaking—an ecstasy summit gives way to generosity, and he'll never remember your I.O.U. Stockbroker types who enjoy doing coke like to feel rich and powerful, so if that's your poison, attend their parties and do their lines. Drugs are much more exciting when you don't pay for them. Buying drugs is more indulgent than purchasing Todd Oldham mules at regular price when you know there is a Todd Oldham sample sale down the street at Barneys.

- *A true Frugal Indulgent cannot and will not afford the luxury of addiction.* Keep drugs a recreational pastime. Remember, you are nouveau pauvre, not nouveau riche.

Profile

THE INFREQUENT DINER

David

David has expensive culinary tastes but, unfortunately, no expense account. Being the grin-and-bear-it type, he endures rice and beans, swallows his Ramen with pride, and eats cheese sandwiches six days a week. Then, armed with the money he saves from eating cheaply, he picks one day to go all out for a real treat—and it isn't always Friday, or payday: He picks a new day each week, usually to reward himself for getting through a productive or particularly bad day, and takes himself to the local bistro for a nice plate of steak frites, complete with glass of cabernet, and a dessert liqueur and crème brulée to cap the meal. He doesn't concern himself with the total price of the meal—he has already made the compromise throughout his week to afford his present seat. Instead, he relaxes, savoring each bite of his French ambrosia, taking in the scenery that surrounds him, filling his head with prideful thoughts, knowing that he alone is responsible for treating himself so well. By the time his high from one good meal wears thin, it is almost time for his next weekly excursion. In the meantime, he can fantasize about food the way others wax nostalgic over great romances come and gone. But unlike making do with memories, David can rendezvous weekly.

Profile

Dining with Diplomats

Lilian and Josh

Lilian's boyfriend, Josh, got tickets for a concert at Lincoln Center's Avery Fisher Hall from a friend who couldn't attend. Josh arranged to pick Lilian up at seven-thirty. In the cab, the two read the tickets and discovered that, because of a United Nations event being held at nearby Alice Tully Hall, their concert had started at seven, not eight, as Josh had assumed. Lilian was ready to tell the driver to turn around, but Josh was all dressed up and wanted someplace to go, and he wanted Lincoln Center to be it. He coaxed Lilian to the door of the diplomatic event and confidently flashed his tickets to the bored ticket taker, who, seeing a well-dressed, smart-looking couple, waved them through. Inside, they were greeted by a metal detector and an armed guard. After passing through the metal detector, each entrant had to have her bag searched. Lilian cringed as she emptied her purse, which contained a pair of gag handcuffs she'd won in a bar and the hacksaw from her jewelry-making kit. Unfazed, the guard nodded her through to the lobby where she and Josh ate hors d'oeuvres and drank champagne with dignitaries from around the world and, inexplicably, Bianca Jagger.

As people filed into the theater, Josh overheard a group of people talking about what a shame it was that two of their party couldn't come. Josh asked if the man wouldn't mind parting with the tickets, as his own seats were lousy. The man happily obliged, and Josh and Lilian enjoyed an extravagant affair for free.

Eileen

She was dreading it, but Eileen had already committed herself to attending June's uppity cocktail party. All of those histrionic young society types would be there, and while Eileen had the perfect cocktail dress for the occasion, her attitude made her feel like she was in drag. At least Linda would be coming too—the two would go together. The two would also decide to drop a hit of ecstasy together, and groove along with the scene. They showed up at June's door—looking extravagant, a bottle of Veuve Cliquot in hand—retrieved glasses of water, and planted themselves on the ottoman. Medication time. Within a half hour, the room was looking velveteen. In their comfy sitting position, the women held court, and each obligatory kiss on the cheek felt especially soft. Work was fine, Eileen said. Yes, I'm still with Jason, answered Linda. Good to see you too, the two said collectively, as they bid each guest adieu. By the end of the party, Eileen and Linda were having the time of their lives, fancying themselves edgy folk for cruising the velvet while perfunctorily performing the social graces so carefully ingrained into their hallucinating brains. Elegant, colorful, sensual, the party became more than tolerable, and June never noticed a thing.

rofile

Strike a Poseur

Diane

Diane has lived in her New York City studio apartment for two years but she still gets occasional calls for the previous tenant, Farquar Stevenson. She gathered from the sorts of messages she received on her answering machine ("Farquar, darling, we're in the New York apartment for Wednesday's shoot. Do come to tea next week, and by all means bring your . . . *friend*") that Mr. Stevenson was a fashion photographer whose talents had elevated him from the tiny apartment and modest tax bracket Diane still enjoyed.

One day Diane read in the *New York Observer* that the Eileen Ford modeling agency had relocated from dowdy midtown to a swanky SoHo loft. When she returned home from work, there was a message inviting Farquar Stevenson to the party being held that night at the new loft. Heroines don't think in moments of crisis, they act. Diane jumped into her little black dress, flagged a cab, and arrived at the event fashionably late.

Once there, she approached the table where uninvited poseurs futilely tried to penetrate the icy security.

"Hello, I'm here with Farquar Stevenson."

"Is he here yet?"

Diane's heart skipped a beat before the woman with the list answered her own question.

"No. But go right on up."

Diane straightened her back, smiled placidly, and glided upstairs.

After a few cocktails at the open bar and enough hors d'oeuvres to call it dinner, Diane worked the crowd, chatting up Eileen Ford herself. When people asked her how she was affiliated with the agency, she told them of her close relationship with Farquar Stevenson ("We met through friends"). When people asked where Farquar was that night, Diane shrugged, "I don't know. It's not like him to miss an event like this, is it?"

Lisa

When Lisa arrived in Los Angeles on vacation, she was wearing the duck boots and lined trench coat that helped her survive Rhode Island winters. Southern California was considerably warmer than New England, but when she tried to score tickets for *The Tonight Show,* she wore her foul-weather gear to set herself apart from the crowd.

And there was a crowd, so Lisa abandoned hopes of getting standby tickets through honest channels. She cut to the front of the line and introduced herself to the ticket dispenser as a reporter from the *Boston Globe.* When asked for her press pass, Lisa said that, like a fool, she'd forgotten it at the hotel. The ticket dispenser, needing verification, offered to call her office to check her identity. Lisa said sure and that it would be easier, given the complex series of extensions to get through, if she dialed the number herself. She dialed her roommate, Karen, and said, "Karen, it's Lisa. I'm here at *The Tonight Show.* They need verification that I work at the paper." She passed the phone to the ticket official to whose few questions

Karen—suddenly the managing editor of the *Globe*—fudged general affirmative answers.

Lisa was ushered to the first row, where she enjoyed the show in the generous shadow of Jay Leno's chin.

THE PLEASURE OF YOUR COMPANY: STAYING IN

Unless your on-the-town activities are on the house, you are better off keeping it in the house. The way to save money and not sacrifice much swank is to be a savvy home entertainer.

Parties

BLOWOUTS. Big bashes are a blast, and they are the easiest type of party to organize. Not as easy as they used to be, mind you. You are an adult now, and you need more than an unfurnished basement and a keg to be entertained.

Parties are perfect opportunities to show off your hosting skills (the drinks, the food, the witty chatter), blow off steam (there will be dancing, of course), and meet new people. And, if you follow a few simple guidelines in preparing for them, your parties will be the toast of the town.

The Right Time. Make it an ordinary Saturday night. You have all day to clean the apartment, go shopping, cook, and primp, and your guests will have had a chance to relax after the workweek and won't be stressed about Monday yet. Tell people the party's at nine. If they know what's what, they'll show after ten.

If you have your heart set on a holiday party, make it an offbeat one, like Arbor Day. People have big expectations for holidays like Halloween or New Year's Eve. Also, friends are less likely to be

double-booked on nonholiday weekends, and are thus less likely to
leave your apartment to party hop with other friends. Nothing is
worse than a mass exodus before midnight.

Check Please. Before you finalize the date, do some market research. Call a few key friends—close friends who won't hold a flop
against you, friends who like to dance, friends who are good conver-
sationalists—to see if they can attend. If you can stack the room with
partygoing assets, the odds of success will be in your favor.

Snackie Treats. For a knock-down-drag-out, the provisions are
simple: an unlimited supply of alcohol and tortilla chips. Unlike
with cocktail parties (see below), food is not high on the list of priorities. Make a few nice dips for chips, and perhaps some chocolate
chip cookies or some brownies, and the kids will be happy. Leave
some things for the last minute—food preparation preferably—and
solicit help from the first guests to arrive. It's good to have a bustle
going at the onset—people chopping vegetables, opening wine, etc.
It ensures that your guests will have something to do and talk about
at the potentially awkward beginning. It also makes them feel a personal interest in the party's success.

Booze. Keep it simple: Make it beer and wine. The mixed-drink
scene will send prices through the roof. You'll need a variety of
liquors and plenty of mixers. If you avoid liquor altogether, no one
will miss it. Consider spicing things up:

Make a pot of something. Make sangria. Make cider. Make
punch. These drinks are festive, they make it look like you exerted
yourself, they often give things a seasonal kick, and they stretch your
booze.

Make it a theme. Have a red wine party to celebrate the arrival of
this year's Beaujolais nouveau. Have a martini party, for which you
do need alcohol, but only gin and vermouth, which makes things
easy. Have a white trash party: Pabst Blue Ribbon all around.

If you serve beer and wine, you need to buy only a starter supply
because people will bring their own. When you invite folks and they

ask what they can bring, say "beer" to half of them and "wine" to the other half.

Decor. If you are going with the basics as far as food and drink are concerned, you ought to funk up the ambience. Give the apartment a wipe-down. You'll have to clean it after the party too, so don't overdo it.

Decorate using some conversation pieces. Memorabilia from your trip to Las Vegas. The wacky album you bought at a garage sale. The self-help flash cards a friend sent you as a joke: These are all things that get people chatting.

Dimmers please. Lighting is paramount to success. Make it not too dark, not too light, but err on the side of the former. Candles and dim lights put forward the best face of even a shabby apartment . . . and a shabby guest.

Furniture. Don't make the mistake of moving all of the furniture to the sides. This creates a wide, threatening space reminiscent of the high school gym before the dances got going. Move furniture as the party heats up.

You. Your appearance reflects your expectations. The guests will take their cues from you. If you want the party to be casual, dress casually. If you want to put on the dog, put on an outfit that says so. Big bashes are theater, so don your costume.

Music. Assign a DJ or make several mix tapes. Music is key—it can fuel the energy of the party.

COCKTAIL PARTIES. A cocktail party is the paradigm of swank. What is more swellegant and adult than mingling with a martini in one hand and a little nibblie thing in the other? Install a baccarat table and you are costarring in a David Niven film.

A cocktail party is held in the early evening, around six or seven, and is meant to last only until nine or ten. If it mutates into a bash that swings until all hours, so much the better. Because most cocktail parties are of short duration, and witty chatter is the preferred activity, flops are rare. But attention to detail is essential. Don't bother throwing a cocktail party if you don't intend to provide decent food and ambience.

Decadence costs, dearies. But there are some corners that can be lopped off without anyone noticing.

Timing. Cocktails are a lovely midweek diversion, say on a Wednesday or Thursday. Don't plan a cocktail party for a weekend night. People end the workweek with the desire to relax and party. Cocktails require too much intellectual energy for guests and hosts alike.

Food. Don't attempt a cocktail party if you are not going to attempt to cook. Cocktail events focus on food because they happen at dinner time. People expect hors d'oeuvres. Creating little bites for such an event is not difficult but it requires preparation and some money.

Now is not the time to show off that flambé dish you've perfected. Stick with foods that can be left on a table for hours and still be tasty at room temperature. Think focaccia, a cheese board with bread and crackers (a.k.a. old faithful), vegetables with an interesting dip or two, fruit, bruschette, cookies, and pasta salad.

Save money by splurging on a nice cheese or two and surrounding the expensive showpieces with seasonal fruit, which is pleasing to the eye and the wallet. We call this a cheap-expensive juxtaposition.

Have the basics ready to go, and something extra up your sleeve. Prepare a delicious plum cobbler or bread pudding ahead of time and put it in the oven after the guests arrive. Pull it out in the middle of the party and watch the crowd go wild. (Or, if you are not a baker and a friend who is calls to ask what to bring, by all means, tell him that a lovely homemade something or other would be much appreciated.)

If you are short on time or culinary talent, spend a few extra bucks for some prepared foods. Buy a panettone (a big, sweet Italian bread, which comes in a box. It's gorgeous and ready to go). Buy a tin of biscotti at a specialty food shop (if the tin is cute, you needn't even remove the biscotti). These things go a long way.

Booze. The liquor cabinet is the big money drain. Unless you have a theme cocktail party (e.g., martinis, gin and tonics, or even wine tasting), you'll have to make an investment. Buy a bartending book—*Mr. Boston* or *The Bartender's Bible*—and a variety of liquors and mixers. There is no way around a significant outlay of cash (or credit) here, but consider these money savers:

- *Throw the party with roommates or a friend or two.* Cosponsorship cuts costs and labor and increases attendance.
- *Let your guests contribute.* When people ask what they can bring, suggest a small bottle of gin, vodka, or scotch. Don't shy away from asking for more than a bottle of wine. Let the party pay for itself.
- *Stock your liquor cabinet.* Because you'll have leftover alcohol, for which you'll only need a few mixers, the next party you have will be much less expensive. Make your cocktail parties regular events and in no time you'll have yourself a little salon.

Music. A cocktail party is the perfect opportunity for you to pull out your collection of retro music—Esquivel, Rosemary Clooney, Tony Bennett; your collection of jazz and blues—Alberta Hunter, Sarah Vaughan, or Thelonious Monk; or your foreign swank, like favorite Edith Piaf. As long as it sings "civilized," you are all set.

Dress Code. As with the food, if you aren't going to go all out (or make it look like you have), you should not host a cocktail party. Part of the fun is dressing up and acknowledging that you are making an effort to please your friends. When else do you have a chance to wear your shiny vintage best?

DINNER PARTIES. If your friends share your frugal indulgent inclinations then they'll be delighted to attend your dinner parties. It's one-stop shopping for free food and fun.

If you enjoy cooking, dinner parties are irresistible. If you're a novice cook, don't be daunted. Dinner parties don't have to be complicated. Your friends will be glad to have anything home cooked and will be flattered to have been one of the small number invited. Here is how to keep the costs under control:

Delegate. If a good cook offers to bring something with him, say yes. Then you won't have to worry about a salad or dessert. When the others ask what to bring, say wine to some and a pint of Ben & Jerry's to others. Suddenly it's a port-à-party and you've got half the work done.

Keep It Simple. Don't overextend yourself. Serve something manageable like a roast chicken (which is very low maintenance but impressive), pasta and salad, chili and corn bread, or a stew with peasant bread. Don't make things that require lots of time and attention. Your guests want to spend as much time with you as with your food.

Keeping it simple enables you actually to pull it off without embarrassment and ensures that costs will be low. None of the above suggestions require you to take on a second job. They are peasant foods whose ingredients cost little and go a long way. Face the facts: You are not Martha Stewart; keep your expectations within the realm of reality.

Hanging Out

Your party can't flop if you don't have one. Semantics are everything. Instead of a "party" have a "get together" or "a few friends over." If there is no label to live up to, friends have no expectations and you can all have a mellow time at the last minute without worrying. There are many ways to have fun in your own backyard.

RENT MOVIES/WATCH TV. Have a bad sequel night and rent things like *Grease 2,* or see if *9 to 5* is on the tube.

PLAY GAMES. Haul out the Scrabble board. A couple of beers later, Scrabble, Pictionary, and Charades rock.

HAVE SEX. A party à deux, sex is the cheapest thrill around. (See Bed Is the Poor Man's Opera, page 143.)

Alone at Last, All Alone

Sometimes the most decadent thing you can do is nothing. Despite the fact that it's Saturday, despite that there are parties you could attend and movies you could see, sometimes it's fun to leave it all behind and stay home to clip your toenails, talk on the phone long distance (after 11 P.M., please), listen to the best of Barry Manilow, and eat Häagen-Dazs. It's hard work being you. Give yourself an occasional break.

Profile

It's My Party, and I'll Tarp the Floors If I Want To

Pamela

Pamela has the mixed blessing of sharing a city with her parents. Once a year, when she has the craving to throw a knock-down-drag-out bash, her parents generously offer their three-story, white-carpeted town house, and take off for the weekend. Pamela rings her sister, and the two get together to plan the list of invitees, the menu, the bar, and quite possibly, the theme. Invitations are sent and R.S.V.P.s are received. The day arrives, and the girls roll out the white carpet, or more accurately, the off-white tarp, and line the carpeting and hardwood floors with the canvas. Next step, type up and print out a guest list. Pamela runs her fingers through her Rolodex and gets friends to volunteer their skills in the following areas: bartending, bouncing, food set up, DJ-ing. Once the various responsibilities have been accepted; the food displayed; the bar fully stocked with Stoli, beer, wine, champagne, and assorted mixers; the music lined up for an evening of dancing; the floors adequately protected; and the psychocrashers deterred, the party begins . . . and fun is had by all. The cleanup is simplicity itself, as Pamela and sib roll up the tarp, shake it out on the street, throw out the Dixie-ware, and wash dishes. Pamela's sister takes the recycling out, the kitchen floor mopped up, the house aired out from the smoke, in time for the 'rents return, as if the party never happened.

Profile

Classified Ad-Minister

TIM

Weddings are notoriously expensive parties. When it's your turn to throw one, let's hope you know people like Tim. When a friend told Tim he was finally going to tie the knot with his girlfriend, Tim wanted to know if there was anything he could do to help, anticipating an invitation to be the best man. Eager to have a casual, secular ceremony, and more important, to avoid shelling out a hundred dollars to tip the minister, the friend asked, "Do you think you could get ordained as a minister of the peace?" Tim was quick to agree to the arrangement—what could be better than best man but the minister? (Ministers don't have to rent tuxedos.) He answered a classified ad he found in the back of *Rolling Stone* for a "church" that would ordain him for only five dollars. Tim picked his own title (The Most Reverend) and his personal church's name (the Congregation-Free Church of Choice), and he was ready to roll. He later officiated at several friends' weddings. For a while, the arrangement worked: The friends paid Tim nothing but praise for his services, and in return Tim got all the free food and drink he could ingest at receptions and rehearsal dinners. But attending wedding after wedding was getting a bit tedious, and Tim was developing a repulsion for rubbery-textured chicken and tame wild rice. After a year, and one minuscule tax break, he closed the book on his ministry and ended up paying full price for a minister at his own wedding.

Lunch Box: The Four Grueling Steps to Actually Cooking for Yourself

"GOOD COOKING IS THE RESULT OF A BALANCE STRUCK BETWEEN FRUGALITY AND LIBERALITY."

—PATIENCE GRAY

It doesn't take a hero to make a decent dinner. (And a decent dinner is *not* a hero.) Cooking for yourself is infinitely less expensive than eating out, and it is easy. If you are good at it, it can be more indulgent, too (see Dinner Parties, page 126). If you are not, follow these four simple steps to become culinarily competent:

1. *Become a vegetarian.* Meat is an expensive, fattening hassle. You don't need it in your life. (The only exception is at an elegant restaurant where a friend is footing the bill. In that case, order the sirloin.) Find a good vegetable market, shop there regularly, and watch your food bills plummet.
2. *Make a few investments.* Buy three simple cookbooks. Cookbooks are worth the small investment. Start with a soup cookbook, a simple vegetarian (or mostly vegetarian) cookbook, and a reliable general book.

   Buy the best ingredients you can find. If a recipe calls for Parmesan cheese, do not buy the one in the green cardboard can. Buy a block of pure, unadulterated Parmesan from a reliable grocer or cheese shop. It is more expensive, but it's worth it: You'll cook with it time and again and the taste will be unparalleled. Since you are picking simple recipes, there probably won't be many ingredients to buy anyway. If there are (as in, say, a stew) the ingredients probably will be inexpensive and easy to find.

Buy some equipment. Nothing fancy—mistrust any recipe that requires new cookware.

3. *Figure out a few recipes.* First read all of the introductory material at the front of the cookbook you are using. (Cookbooks are books; they *can* be read.) Then find a few of the easiest recipes (don't be overambitious) and set aside time to practice preparing them. Make this a leisure activity on a Saturday. Someday not too far down the road, you can try them on friends. (Your friends will be impressed by your command of peasant cuisine.) Then you can branch out, trying new recipes and creative variations on old ones.

4. *Keep it simple and relax.* Follow the directions closely, and don't worry about the results. If you use good ingredients, the dishes you make are certain to be decent, if not better than takeout. Besides, if something you make is truly bad, you'll eat it anyway because you slaved over it, it's cheap, it's nutritious, and there's nothing to be embarrassed about; you are in your own home and nobody will know you ate badly prepared slop. If a soufflé falls in the oven with nobody around, does anybody hear it? No.

DATING: A SHOT IN THE DARK

"I WANT SOMEBODY WHO WILL EITHER PUT OUT FOR ME OR PUT ME
OUT OF MY MISERY."

—ANI DIFRANCO, "ASKING TOO MUCH"

Love may be a many splendored thing, but a Frugal Indulgent also seeks the splendor of paid dinners, gifts, free entertainment, rent and bills split two ways, and the like. There are two ways to go about this: dating and having a relationship. Which suits your needs better? To answer this, first think about this question: When you need ten dollars, do you ask ten people for a dollar, or one person for ten? If you find asking ten people for one dollar more appealing, you enjoy dating. If you prefer getting it all from one pal, you are a relationship hound. If you spread your needs among ten people, you are not expected to reimburse, whereas if you exploit one source for the entire amount, you should reciprocate the favor.

In this section, we will explore the financial implications of dating and relationships. You can be wined and dined for weeks by numerous charming escorts, and not spend a dime. Or, you can split your living costs with one true love. Here are some thoughts to keep in mind before we begin:

- *Don't ask, don't pay.* Whether you are gay or straight, male or female, here's the protocol for gracious dating in the nineties: If you ask someone out, you pay the bill. Turn the charm dial to eleven, and seduce your love prospect into seducing you. Get all of the responsibility out of your lap and into someone else's.
- *Aim high.* Date people who are in a higher tax bracket than you. At the very least, your escort will prorate the cost, if not absorb the whole bill. Chances are their tastes will match their high incomes, and you will be treated to culture.

- *Time is money.* Seeing older people has its perks as well. One would hope these people are more advanced in their careers than you are, so expect salaries commensurate with experience and hitch your wagon to that star.
- *"Bed is the poor man's opera."* Whether you date rich or poor, there is one form of entertainment that should always be satisfying, and should always be free (minus the negligible cost of a box of condoms): sex. Have it, and often.
- *Breaking up is hard to do.* Sudden solitude is expensive. When you've grown accustomed to her face and finances, it's hard to let go. No more free rides. No more prorated or divided expenses. Moving costs. There is nothing sweet about the sorrow of parting.

TO HAVE AND HAVE NOT: DATING VS. RELATIONSHIPS

Once you have gotten over the fact that you are no different from your forebears, for whom coupling was an economic necessity—determining where boundaries were drawn and to whom their estates were passed—you can get down to business. The business of romance involves strategic planning. Before you do anything else, determine your goals. Are you interested in a short-term tryst, or a long-term commitment? Read on. Here we offer the balance sheet on dating versus committing.

Note: *People who tell you that dating for dollars is crass and opportunistic are trapped in a romantic dream state. Welcome to the age of reason.*

Dating Pros

Serial dating is ideal for those who value high-risk, short-term investments and who worry about cash flow. By going out with many different people you'll increase your options and see a lot of revenue coming in from many sources.

A DIVERSIFIED PORTFOLIO. Dating exposes you to a broad range of people and experiences. You'll escape the worry that your eggs are all in one basket, and you won't slip easily into any ruts. And there are bonuses:

Dinner. Dining out is one of the most popular dating activities, especially between people who don't know each other well. The idea is that they'll loosen up over a bottle of merlot, chat, and become acquainted. It works. After a while, the dining daters become a couple and lose interest in going out. After he's taken you out, say, three times, he may think he can skimp with movie rentals and Rollerblading. When the law of diminishing returns sets in, it's time to make a decision: Move on to the next one (for more free dinners), make a move on him (see "Bed Is the Poor Man's Opera," page 143), or move into his rent-controlled apartment.

Movies/Plays. Watching other people talk rather than having to do so yourselves (as on a dinner date) can be a relief. Movies are perfect venues for boring or taciturn dates. If you get the sense that your date has plentiful cash reserves, up the ante from cinema to theater.

REAL ESTATE. The more people you date, the greater your chances of spending time away from the city at a variety of parents' and friends' country houses. Dating is like a great big Monopoly game: See how many spaces you can land on without paying rent.

CONTACTS. Invitation multiplication happens when you are on the market. Single people go to more parties than their coupled friends. They meet more people, eat more free food, drink at more open bars, and get invited to yet more parties. Single people invite single friends out more often than they do coupled ones because (1) single friends reciprocate, (2) single friends stay out later, and (3) single people assume that couples would rather be home curled up in front of the television even if they don't have cable.

Dating Cons

DEPLETION OF NATURAL RESOURCES. On the other hand, constantly going out can be a drain.

Energy. It takes work to be *on* all the time. Sometimes it's nice to switch to autopilot. If there is someone waiting for you at the cave, you don't feel like a hermit, even at your most antisocial.

Time. Managing a full social calendar, which includes drumming up dates, worrying about them, and actually going on them is difficult to coordinate. If you feel there isn't enough time in the day or room in your Filofax, that's because, indeed, there isn't.

Cash Reserves. Dating depletes cash reserves even if other people pay for most things. You've still got to have the wardrobe, the cab fare, the housewarming presents, etc.

Relationship Pros

We have been informed by those who know it well that commitment is a cost-cutting measure. If you feel comfortable buying futures, shop around for a relationship that is built to last.

COST-CUTTING. You cut your food, utility, and magazine subscription bills in half.

INCREASED ASSETS. You double your CD collection, cookware, furniture, sometimes even your wardrobe.

PERKS. Entertainment becomes reliable and cheap—staying in is okay when you can count on sex.

DIVISION OF LABOR. Someone has to stay home to wait for the cable guy, clean the bathtub, take out the newspapers. At last there is twice the likelihood it won't have to be you anymore.

Relationship Cons

DOWNSIZING. Your social life declines somewhat when you couple. For many this is a blessing; for the gregarious among us it's a curse. If variety is the spice of life, then you are looking at a lifetime of mashed potatoes.

DISSOLUTION. There is always the risk that your partnership will crumble. You will then have to face the prospect of losing half your assets. Tangibles like CDs, books, and clothes, as well as intangibles like friends and favorite restaurants, will have to be divvied up. When you cross the great divide, there are also new costs incurred: moving costs, therapy, the cost of a new phone hookup, etc. Beware: A break in your relationship may also break your bank.

MEET MARKET: HOW TO FIND FRESH BLOOD

"WE ARE ALL IN THIS TOGETHER—BY OURSELVES."

—LILY TOMLIN

Whether you need a temp for a few dates or you are looking for love, you've got to peel yourself off the futon and get on the scene. While breaking up may be hard to do, these days getting together may be even more difficult. How do you go about finding someone who is perfect for you? The traditional methods still work and there are newer ones that are becoming even more popular.

The Easy Way Out

FRIENDS OF FRIENDS. Ask people who are dating how they met. The most common response you hear is "through a mutual friend." When you attend a party, always take a guest, and expect that he or she will reciprocate the favor. Be careful with friends of friends: Don't embarrass yourself in front of them because it will come back to you like a boomerang. When you date friends of friends, you get to meet people who may be outside of your field, which is nice because they may be bankers who want to take you for decent meals and pay for everything.

CO-WORKERS. This can get sticky. Don't kid yourself: Other people at the office will find out. If you have a bad breakup you still must see the person all the livelong day. On the upside, the two of you might have similar interests and similar salaries.

PEOPLE IN YOUR FIELD. Think of trade shows as very big mixers. They are like cocktail parties to which you don't have to bring a bottle of wine. If you don't get to go to the show yet, try to go to your industry's smaller social events. If not a date, you may at least get a free dinner off the nibblie tray.

EX-LOVERS. It's a lot easier to fall back than it is to propel yourself forward, which is why ex-lovers make such appealing game. You don't have to summarize your life over dinner with them, and you both tend to be more relaxed. On the downside, there's probably a good reason you broke up. Don't kid yourself: Call a spade a spade and make the relapse a one-nighter.

On the Desperate Hand

Desperate circumstances call for desperate measures: Looking to friends, co-workers, and the past is not always enough to find a suitable date. Sometimes you've got to hit the streets and do some hardcore shopping.

BARS. When you meet someone in a bar you know that he's got one thing in common with you: He drinks. Is that enough for a relationship? Maybe for some, but not the picky among us. Hanging out in a bar until you meet someone costs a lot of money and time. It's not worth going out of your way. If you spend lots of time in bars anyway, then it's worth it to keep your eyes peeled.

FIX-UPS. At first people are squeamish about being fixed up. It seems too brazen, too deliberate. Then they hit a certain point in a mediocre dating career and get over it. It may be deliberate, but it cuts to the chase. And with hand-picked partners, there is more likelihood of finding a match. It helps to have ruthless, meddling friends who are willing to rack their Rolodexes on behalf of your libido.

PERSONALS. Some people we know have had great luck with this very controlled, methodical—yet fun—way of fishing. It requires great stamina, but not a lot of money. Ad rates vary from city to city, but are reasonable for the remarkable results they generate. Be the placer of the ad and spell out your needs. That way, you have control over: the cost of the date, how high-maintenance it is, and whom you want to respond to. Make the meetings café dates, which are cheap and quick. Save your strength for the deluge. Ads can generate hundreds of responses.

MEDDLING RELATIONS. Your parents want to feel involved in your life? Fine. Let them find you someone to date. They love little projects that keep them busy and feeling in the loop. Your mom's college roommate's son lives two blocks from you? Have drinks with him. You have nothing to lose but some free time.

RANDOM. A girl stops you on the street and asks you out. A fellow book-buyer invites you to have coffee with him. Do you accept? If he looks okay, why not? You take his card and call him to arrange it. That way, you are in control. If you give him your number, make it the office number. You'll meet for the date in a public place, size him up, maybe have a friend swing by the café to "bump into you" and later offer a second opinion.

Profile

Pass It On

Sarah and Janice

Every morning, Sarah saw the same nice-looking, well-dressed guy smiling at her on the subway. One day he approached her and asked her out on a date. Sarah wasn't in the market for a relationship at the time and she told him so. Then, because he seemed so nice, attractive, and willing, she asked him if she could give his number to one of her friends whom she thought he'd like.

She gave his number to Janice, Janice gave him a call, and the two lived happily ever after, at least for a night.

Profile

Spelling It Out

Angelina

Tired of not meeting any decent men, Angelina decided to lay it on the line. She placed a personal ad in the *Boston Phoenix* and *Boston Globe* indicating that she was a hot Latina mama looking for fun. The responses flooded in. She spent a year screening the applicants, dating some, and placing a few more ads—some with more subdued language. Finally, she responded to one of the respondents, Michael. They dated, fell in love, and now live in wedded bliss.

"BED IS THE POOR MAN'S OPERA": SEX

"IF YOU WANT IT, HERE IT IS, COME AND GET IT, BUT YOU BETTER
HURRY 'CAUSE IT'S GOING FAST."

—BADFINGER, "IF YOU WANT IT"

You can get a friend to take you to dinner. You can take in a free concert in the park. You can go the local dive bar and down some domestic beer. You can treat yourself and a friend to lunch on your expense account. You can have a Blockbuster night with a college crony. But, let's admit it—sometimes you need a little something more to put that spring in your step. We have something in mind, and guess what? It is absolutely free.

It is, of course, sex. It can be tremendously satisfying, rather exciting, a cure-all for physical and psychic pain, and downright entertaining. It can also provide a shit-eating grin and give way to lots of gossip. But most important, it can give you a darn good orgasm at the hands of another, and you don't have to pay a dime.

The hard part, of course, is finding a willing participant. Love may take luck, but sex is just a fuck, and doesn't necessarily take too much skill to procure. You're fabulous, you give conversation like so much great foreplay—you've got it going on. For now, we will pay homage to the cheapest thrill around.

Okay, condoms cost money. They are, however, a good thing to have around (beware the rubber in the wallet or back pocket— unlike Hostess Twinkies, they don't have a shelf-life spanning a century) and well worth the small price. Sex toys and other accoutrements tend to cost hundreds of dollars, so seek those people who have access to the things you need and desire (unless of course fetish objects like a rubber suit are your indulgences, in which case, you can write them off as worthy investments). If your amour du jour is also a Frugal Indulgent with a taste for the decadent, there are cheap alternatives. Bondage can be fun using pantyhose and neckties for blindfolds and tie-ups. (We advise against clotheslines, and other ropy materials; they leave marks, and rope burns hurt like hell.) Straight couples may enjoy the kink of swapping underwear, which costs nothing. Dick might feel fabulous wearing Jane's Victoria's Secret panties under his tweed suit, and Jane might love the little trapdoor in Dick's BVDs, especially under her DKNY hose.

Whatever your pleasure, even sex allows you to FYI without squelching your lusty desires. So whether you're your own best lay, or whether you get the satisfaction you need from a Dick or Jane, even a pauper can afford the most decadent sex, so go to the poor man's opera.

Vacation

All I Ever Wanted

"IF THE ADVENTURES WILL NOT BEFALL A YOUNG LADY IN HER
OWN VILLAGE, SHE MUST SEEK THEM ABROAD."
—JANE AUSTEN, *NORTHANGER ABBEY*

Is there anything more decadent than leisure? Free time and the
mind-set to enjoy it are what having a low-paying job buys you.
When it comes time to relax, poverty is worth every penny. You
don't have to worry about who is holding down the fort; you don't
have to bring your cellular phone with you or call in to the voice mail
every half hour.

Nowhere is the chasm between scrimping and splurging more
dramatic than in vacations. For some people, taking off from work
is vacation enough; for others, taking off in a jumbo jet is the only
way to justify calling it a vacation. There are many ways to make a
vacation happy.

What Frugal Indulgent travel really boils down to is a basic decision: Are you going to slum it or are you going in style? You probably already know how to slum. Slumming involves accepting that
you have little money and trying to make that small stash last by
spending as little of it as possible. Kerry took off for Costa Rica,
where she slept on beaches and ate lots of beans and rice. Jason went
camping. Kera never left her apartment except to buy food and cig-

arettes and rent videos. Traveling in style involves acting financially endowed. It involves charging the European airfare and worrying about it later; using the resources of friends to one's own advantage; and using one's charm, wiles, and little white lies to cajole favors from wealthy strangers. If you want to swank it up on the road remember this: It is easier to hitch a free ride on a Lear jet than it is on a Greyhound.

THE TRAVEL QUIZ

1 Rate the following scenarios according to their palatability (one being highest):

a) Your parents are going to Hilton Head for three weeks to explore the possibility of living there upon their imminent retirement. They invite you and your sister to spend the week between Christmas and New Year's, but you and your sib must share one of the two double beds in your parents' hotel room.

b) Your parents invite you and your sister to spend the week between Christmas and New Year's with them at your childhood summer home in Hilton Head.

c) Your parents are going to Hilton Head for three weeks to explore the possibility of living there upon their imminent retirement. They invite you and your lover to spend the week between Christmas and New Year's with them in their small two-bedroom condo. Because they are your parents, one of you will have to take the living room couch.

d) Your parents invite you, your lover, and your sister to spend the week between Christmas and New Year's with them at your childhood summer home in Hilton Head.

2. Match Game: Pair the list of major airlines at left with their frequent flyer mileage partners at right.

A) USAir
B) United
C) Delta
D) TWA
E) Virgin
F) Northwest
G) Continental

1) British Airways, Air France, Alitalia, JAL, Northwest, Qantas, Sabena, Swissair
2) Air Canada, Great Lakes Aviation, Aloha, Aeromar, Air France, ALM, Cayman Airways, SAS (Scandinavia), TWA Express
3) Swissair, Singapore Airlines, Mexicana, Air New Zealand, Austrian Airlines
4) Air India, Alaska Airlines, Philippine Airlines
5) Midwest Express, British Midland
6) KLM, Air New Zealand, Alaska Airlines, America West, Midwest Express, USAir
7) Iberia, Aer Lingus, Alitalia, America West, Malaysia, Qantas, SAS

3. Complete the following sentence: When I have three consecutive days off from work I go to:

a) see my best friend in a nearby city
b) visit my parents
c) the supermarket and laundromat
d) the office
e) Mallorca

4 Baggage Claim: You are going to Barcelona for five days at the beginning of November. Four identical suitcases fall out of the overhead compartment. Yours is the one that contains:

a) a pair of jeans, one dressy item, a pair of shoes, six pairs of underwear, six pairs of socks, one sweater, three long-sleeve T-shirts, a thin foldup raincoat, a toothbrush, antiperspirant, traveler's checks

b) a pair of jeans, one dressy item, a pair of shoes, six pairs of underwear, six pairs of socks, one sweater, three long-sleeve T-shirts, a thin foldup raincoat, a toothbrush, antiperspirant, cash

c) a pair of jeans, one dressy item, a pair of shoes, six pairs of underwear, six pairs of socks, one sweater, three long-sleeve T-shirts, a thin foldup raincoat, a toothbrush, antiperspirant, credit cards

d) a pair of jeans, one dressy item, a pair of shoes, six pairs of underwear, six pairs of socks, one sweater, three long-sleeve T-shirts, a thin foldup raincoat, a toothbrush, antiperspirant

5 It is August, and New York City has become Gotham Inferno. Your air conditioning doesn't work. Your passport has expired and due to a government shutdown, you can't renew it before your upcoming two weeks off. You must scrap your plans for border crossing and do something domestic. What is your plan?

a) Stay at your friend's share in Easthampton for a week.

b) Go to a B&B with a friend for a long weekend in Spring Lake, New Jersey.

c) Rent a car and take a two-week road trip with a friend who is on a life deferral plan and can spare big chunks of time to go to Moosehead Lake, Maine.

d) Have a New York City vacation hanging around at pleasantly air conditioned museums, movie theaters, and automatic teller machine vestibules.

e) Visit a friend in Atlanta.

ANSWERS:

1. Three points for **b**. It's not the best vacation in the world but it's the least of four evils. That it is a summer home versus a childhood home makes it more appealing. Everyone's on vacation, and there's less to fight about. Two points if you chose **d**. Your lover acts as a buffer and your sister acts as a playmate to you both. One point for **a**. Things are pretty crowded. Sharing a bedroom with Mom and Dad leaves something to be desired, but since you are all on vacation in a new spot, things may not be as tense as usual and you may all have some laughs. No points for **c**. You are an adult now. If you want to have a nice vacation with your lover, spend the money and get your own place. Visit Mom and Dad on Christmas day, then take off for a quaint B&B together.

2. A=1, B=2, C=3, D=4, E=5, F=6, G=7. Memorize these partnerships. If you pick your frequent flyer plan wisely you will maximize your miles. (See A Few Words about Frequent Flying, page 183.)

3. Four points for **a**. Three days at a best friend's place is ideal. The perfect company, the perfect length of time. Three points for **c**. It's important to nurture yourself sometimes. A three-day weekend is a great way to unwind, run low-key errands, and treat yourself to clean sheets and tasty home-cooked food. Note: If it were a week, staying at home would be a waste. Two points for **e**.

If you had five days, or even four, in a row this would be the clear winner. But by the time you get there, you'll have to come right home. Still beats the hell out of other options. One point for **b**. If you haven't seen them in a while, three days is long enough for a quality visit and, in most cases, not long enough to spark a family feud. But it can be stressful and draining. May not be worth the travel and expense. No points for **d**. It's okay to go to the office on a regular weekend. When there are three in a row, seize the days.

4. Yours is the suitcase that contains no money. Three points for **d**. Your wallet belongs on your person—luggage routinely gets lost. All of the other answers are very bad, but in case you did choose one of them, here's how they break down. Two points for **b**. If your cash is in your bag, we hope your credit cards are on you. Cash is the thing to bring on a short trip. Why waste time changing traveler's checks when you have no time to spare? One point for **c**. If your credit cards are in your bag, we hope your cash is on you. Credit cards are always a must on a trip, whether it is to the grocery store or to Barcelona. No points for **a**. Don't bring traveler's checks on a short trip. Bring cash and credit cards; if you don't lose money at home, chances are you won't lose it abroad.

5. Four points for **a**. Country home crashing is a fine skill, and you deserve a pat on the back for your ability to hone it. You'll hardly spend any money and all you'll have to do is be charming, flexible, and a willing dish washer. Three points for **c**. You have a friend with you so you will experience shared laughs on your adventure. You'll go to HoJo's and visit silly sites, and you'll split the costs of rooming, which won't be too bad in the north country. Two points for **b**. Spring Lake is pretty, but the B&Bs cost bucks at that time of year, and it's a bit crowded on the beach. One point for **e**. Hotlanta is as hopping a music scene as it is a steamy clime in Au-

gust. But you'll get away, there's lots of a/c in that town, and you won't spend too much money on off-season airfare. No points for **d.** You might as well just stay in the office rather than cruise for air conditioning in this way. Okay for a weekend, tired by Tuesday.

TAKING THE EASY WAY OUT: DAY-TRIPPING

Day trips are to people with jobs what road trips are to slackers—a chance to have a change of scene and perhaps an adventure. So hit the local road.

A Day in the Country

BE KIND TO YOUR CAR-OWNING FRIENDS. The key to successful day-tripping is car possession. If you don't own, try to borrow. Either invite the car owner along, borrow his vehicle, or rent a car. If you rent a car, take public transportation to the suburbs and rent it there where it will be much cheaper. Put it on your gold credit card, which usually covers the insurance, then fill the car to capacity so each person's share will be minimal. If you take a bus or a train, you risk getting stranded—an adventure, yes, but also an expensive hassle.

WHERE TO GO? WHAT TO DO? The annoying thing about a day trip is the planning. If you jet off to Paris for the weekend, you are bound to have a good time no matter where you go and what you do. It's Paris. If you hop in the car and head to Bucks County, Pennsylvania, you might not stumble upon much of interest if you haven't done some preliminary research.

Books. There are books available about day trips in nearly every American city. If you are an avid day or weekend tripper they are worth the investment. If you plan on going just once bring a discreet pad to jot some notes in the back of the bookstore. After one bout of research you'll remember to clip those local newspaper features for the next trip.

People. Do you have a friend in the city or your office who can make recommendations? Natives have the best advice. Make one draw you a map, write down a few restaurants, and recommend a B&B if you are overnighting it.

Pilgrimage. Pick an odd spot and try to find it. Gary and a friend were bored one Sunday so they decided to find Jack Kerouac's grave. They trucked down from Boston to Lowell, Massachusetts, and just drove around the town until they found a memorial park dedicated to the writer. Then they cruised around the town thinking about Jack, wondering how ugly Lowell had spawned his genius, and as soon as they'd sated their beatnik jones, they returned home.

For many people, pilgrimages involve warehouse shopping. Every city transplant knows that the suburbs have the bargains. Consider: Loehmann's, T.J.Maxx, Filene's Basement, Ikea, etc. Yes, these stores are available in cities too, but they are never as good as their suburban siblings.

Pilgrimages can be made on a larger scale too, but save for certain circumstances (see "Profile: They're Going to Graceland," page 173), you don't want to pay oodles of money to ride a one-trick pony.

Wing and a Prayer. If getting there is more than half the fun for you, or if you are going for an out-of-town tryst with a lover, just get in the car and drive. This can be done without fear of boredom along either coast, but some cities' outer limits are disappointing. Ever driven around Toronto? We didn't think so.

The Beautiful Briny Sea

More exotic than a day in the country is a day on the ocean blue. Yachting is, believe it or not, one of the least expensive indulgences you'll find. If you feel like a free ride on a fast boat, go early in the morning to the local yacht club. Chat up the people you find there to see if there is a sailing race that day. Then offer yourself up to the sailors. More often than not, your weight is a welcome addition to a racing boat. You'll get to hang out on the high seas all day, be fed, and probably have drinks bought for you at the club after you return to the marina.

If you decide you like day-tripping on others' yachts, consider a longer trip. For races from, say, Long Island to Bermuda, the sailors usually ride the boat in only one direction and fly back. It is pretty easy to hitch a ride on the empty boat for its weeklong return. All this takes is some prior knowledge of the schedules, which can be learned at the yacht club or in magazines on cruising whose classified ads are particularly revealing.

I WAS JUST IN THE NEIGHBORHOOD: VISITING FRIENDS

If you haven't your own resources for vacation, use those of your friends. Chances are they have cars (or subway savvy), apartments with comfy futon couches, and enough free time to make you dinner and hang out. They may also live in places far enough away that you can make the trip feel foreign and exotic. Let's face it: If you're from Chicago, Los Angeles may as well be on another planet.

There are numerous advantages to visiting friends. You get to catch up with them, of course; you can get away without buying a guidebook and expect that your friend will either show you around or make suggestions; and you pay only for travel and some food. The downside: the feeling of being just a little underfoot, that bar in the middle of the pull-out couch, and the slight loss of freedom that comes with being a houseguest.

Here's how to make it work to everyone's advantage:

- *Do unto others and all that.* The easiest way to be a good houseguest is to put yourself in the host's place. Install yourself not only in his apartment, but in his mind as well. (See Mi Casa, Su Casa: Dealing with Houseguests, page 41.) Think, "If I were [your friend's name] how long would I want to have to trip over someone's luggage in the living room?" "Would I want to have to pay for another person's long-distance phone calls?" "Would I want to have to take a vacation day to visit the National Monument again?" Your answers may shock you.
- *Be solicitous, not obsequious.* Bring a gift. Express delight at seeing your friend. Thank her for her gracious hospitality and use of the car while she's at work. Offer to help make dinner and wash the dishes and so on. But don't overdo it. Nothing highlights your omnipresent underfoot state like frequent gushing reminders of it from your own tongue.
- *Be independent.* You'll be less of a burden if you've brought your own agenda. Of course you'll want to spend lots of time with your friend, but remember that he may want some time alone. He may also not want to have to visit Ellis Island again, see *Cats,* take many days off from work, or eat out every night of your visit. You are the only one in vacation mode.
- *Offer to cook.* You'll save even more money and relieve your host if you encourage eating in during your visit. One of the most frightening things about hosting is the amount of money it takes to keep up with the vacationer who can afford to be prodigal because he's saving so much money staying with you.

DISCRETION ADVISED: PARENTAL VISITS

It looks so enticing: Free room and board, maybe transportation too. Maybe a dog to adore you, a sibling to hang with. There's nostalgia, and—if you haven't seen them in a while—the sort of victory parade treatment offered conquering emperors returning from battle that makes siblings still living at home sick.

Do not be fooled! Were the high school years the best of your life? Then why rush back to the place where they happened? Carefully weigh the following pros and cons before you buy that nonrefundable ticket.

Parental Visit Pros

GROWN-UP TREATMENT. The thrill of feeling like an adult as Mom and Dad eagerly push whiskey sours on you (as though you haven't been drinking since sophomore year in high school) and ask for your two cents on what can be done to squelch the rebellion of your rascally younger brother (as though living away from home has given you new insight on or interest in child rearing).

MAKING MOM AND DAD HAPPY. That proud look in their eyes you haven't seen since right before the big fight at graduation makes it worth dropping by now and then.

MAKING THE DOG HAPPY. Here's love even more unconditional than that of your parents, and someone to sleep with. Realize that the dog is like an inexpensive personal trainer. He's always prodding you to go for a walk or a run. Take him up on the exercise offer.

ARCHIVE MAINTENANCE. Return often enough to ensure that nobody's touched your stuff. Who knows when you'll need to refer to the research you used for your thesis on Byzantium. Important: Never leave a journal of any kind in your parents' care. Remove to your apartment or destroy.

GOODS. Shopping for clothes with Mom, CDs with Dad. Arrive at your parents' home looking shabby enough to make your mother want to treat you to new clothing, but nice enough that she won't be embarrassed to take you to that new restaurant.

SERVICES. Free room, housekeeping facilities, car service, complimentary meals.

SPA/ARTIST'S COLONY. If your parents are low maintenance you may be able to catch up on that sleep and finish your novel.

Parental Visit Cons

LONELINESS, NOSTALGIC DEPRESSION, ENNUI. You're not the only one who's changed. Friends have moved away. New buildings have gone up; others have been torn down. Sometimes a childhood home doesn't live up to your rose-colored memories. You may find you have little to do other than knock around the house and rent movies. Is it worth risking social whiplash as your life screeches to a halt for the duration of your visit?

INFANTILIZATION. Your parents will lapse into old patterns of behavior. As much as they treat you like an adult they'll also treat you like a child. They'll remind you to stop at red lights; criticize your lifestyle choices, appearance, table manners—anything to be parental. Some people we know have even been grounded on a weekend visit.

Combat infantilization by bringing a buffer home with you. A buffer is any stranger in front of whom your family must be polite. The ideal buffer is your latest love interest; nothing puts parents on their best behavior like a new lover. (See Profile: 'Rent Control, page 164.)

REGRESSION. You will lapse into old patterns of behavior. You may catch yourself whining to get your way, fighting with siblings over the car, "calling" for the bathroom/phone/front seat/remote control. Are you behaving like a child because people are treating you like one or vice versa? It's hard to find the beginning of this vicious circle.

MEDDLING. At home you face scrutiny: career inquiries, love life examination, hair advice, clothing evaluation, and comparison to perfect siblings. At hotels they just want your signature.

HOME ALONE: THE DOMESTIC VACATION

Sometimes a person needs to use up vacation time, but has no funds to send her flying. This predicament leads the thwarted traveler to take a domestic vacation. She plans to explore her own city, do errands, sleep in, catch up with friends over relaxing coffees and dinner dates.

If the vacation only spans a few days, this is a reasonable plan; indeed, it may be a welcome retreat. But if the vacation adds up to a week's time, depression replaces novelty and plans dissolve. The lethargy brought on by too much sleep throws the vacationer's body out of whack, and prevents day-tripping. Museums are not visited, matinees are missed, dinners are canceled, and these activities are replaced with unnecessary catnaps (following fourteen-hour sleep cycles) and countless hours in front of the tube. Friends who swore they would hang during your time off get overwhelmed with work, and bail. The domestic vacationer develops new friends: Geraldo, Rolonda, Lucy and Ricky, the Young and the Restless. Eyes glaze. Atrophy overwhelms.

It isn't worth it. Returning to work becomes appealing because, from your island of ennui, your job looks like a haven of camaraderie. Don't let this happen to you. If you have a week off, get out of town, even if it is just for a few days, even if it is just to the neighboring town. You'll feel a lot more relaxed upon your return to your cubicle.

Profile

An Awfully Great Adventure

SUZANNE

Washington, D.C., resident Suzanne radiates bouviessence. She is always dressed and coifed to elegant perfection—friends know JBKO's posthumous gaze proudly smiles on Suzanne. Bearing this in mind, it would seem that when Suzanne was given a week of vacation at the last minute, she should have been the first to book a flight to the French Riviera. About to start a new job the following Monday, Suzanne didn't want to disrupt her week of relaxation with complicated travel plans, but she didn't want to remain idle in the city either. After some contemplation, she set off for Busch Gardens in the neighboring state of Virginia, where she looked forward to kitschy fun in the form of water rides, roller coasters, cotton candy, and historic reenactments of colonial times.

Up on Top of the World

Evie

When Evie's parents came to town for a convention, their hotel room was all wrong. They expressed their dissatisfaction forcefully and effectively; in no time they were upgraded to the only remaining space in the hotel: the Presidential Suite. Evie took one look at the massive suite of rooms and its perks: open bar, little nibblie things, wraparound views, and quickly took action. First she fetched her bags and moved in for a cushy weekend away from her cramped apartment. Then, being an altruistic conservationist who hates to see anything go to waste, she leapt to the phone. She called all her friends and urged them to drop everything and come over for an impromptu party. She shuffled her parents into their rooms for the night, tucked them in, and let the party begin. Friends flocked in from all directions to rock the top of the luxury hotel.

LIKE BEING THERE: VICARIOUS VACATIONS

If you have neither the time nor the money to go someplace fun, travel on the wings of fancy. Vicarious travel is to vacationing what infauxmation (see Cultured Pearls of Wisdom, page 100) is to living. You don't need to have sipped Bellinis by the Grand Canal to know that Venice's Cipriani is the place to do so. You needn't have been to Ireland's tiny town of Sligo to know that the best pizza on the Emerald Isle is made by a nun there. You just need to embrace the media that surrounds you and use your imagination.

Audio-Visual Stimulation

Movies, CDs, CD-ROMS, and the Internet are not like being there, but they're pretty good for a fraction of the time and expense. Go to Rome with Marcello Mastroianni via Fellini. Take a tour of the Louvre without leaving your chair, care of its CD-ROM. Go on a tour of Scotland's scotch breweries—they have a decent web page. Take caution—this sort of behavior may act more as appetizer than entree and leave you unsatisfied and yearning for more.

Books and Magazines

Reading is the way to go. It leaves room for the imagination. Travel magazines and books are fine, but the best way to experience a foreign culture is through the food. Read cookbooks; read *Gourmet* magazine. Can't spare the money for a trip to Provence just now? Bake a fig tart and sip pastis. Bring Italy to your own kitchen by whipping up some gnocchi and sage butter sauce. The caviar dotting your blini is more expensive than what you usually eat, but it sure looks cheap next to a round-trip plane ticket to Moscow.

Quickie

If you need a quickie, try this: Open your Rolodex to *A* and, starting with American Airlines, call all of the 800 numbers of the major airlines and check prices. It takes only about a half an hour to spot-check all of Europe and is nearly as invigorating as a trip there.

These techniques are not quite as good as being abroad, but the upside is rewarding: no waiting at baggage claim, no embarrassing language blunders, and little money spent. Best of all, the food is much better than what you get on the airplane.

Your Friendly Neighborhood Hotel

Hotels are one of the best free resources in town. Do not overlook their wide-ranging amenities just because you are not a paying guest. Look at what you can find if you take the time to investigate:

Information

The concierge is paid to help people. Let him help you. Want to know if there is any good jazz playing tonight but forgot to buy the paper? Need tickets to that sold-out concert? Give the concierge at the local hotel a call and ask for his recommendations. Choose a luxury hotel. Nicer hotels have nicer, more accommodating staffs.

Services

Want to join a gym, but the rates at the independents are too expensive? Call the hotel nearest you and see if they offer memberships to locals. Many have good deals. Don't go to the nicer hotels for this—the midlevel or inexpensive ones are better bets.

Need a ride to the airport? Shuttles leave from most hotels all day long. There are rarely lines for them, you wait in air-conditioned comfort, and the price is the same as what you'd find at the train or bus station.

Having trouble hailing a cab? Ask the doorman to oblige.

Bars

Hotel bars are perfect for romantic assignations. They offer the thrill of feeling far away and usually provide free munchies with drinks. Opt for hotels with rooftop gardens or high, wraparound windows.

Profile

A House in the Country

JEN

Jen's sister Susy used to live in Sunderland, Massachusetts, a charming small town near Amherst, located a mere four hours by bus from Jen's New York City apartment. Whenever the weather was nice, Jen and myriad combinations of her friends and roommates would pile into a Greyhound and escape to Susy's apartment, which Jen had dubbed "My Country Home." At first, Susy thought Jen wanted to spend an unprecedented amount of quality time with her, but when Jen asked Susy to just leave the keys to the house and car on a weekend that Susy had plans to be away, the situation became clear. At first Susy's feathers were ruffled at the notion that her sister might like her apartment more than her, but she relaxed when she realized she could do the same. Now the two both enjoy their cozy apartment exchange program.

Profile

'Rent Control

Kera

Kera is twenty-six and works at a Manhattan publishing house. On the first day of her annual four-day visit home to her parents' house in Chicago, she found herself grounded for the duration of her trip. The trouble began when her parents picked her up at the airport. Upon entering their car, she was bombarded with information about everyone she never cared about. As the car pulled up the driveway, the gossip was continuing with more intensity and no sign of future pause. At the house Kera found out that her room had been rented to someone on a homestay from Brazil. When she went downstairs to get horizontal on the couch in the rec room, Dad advised her of his need to work on the computer and watch TV there. A fight ensued. After a short, high volume embroilment, Kera found herself grounded for the remainder of her stay. No phone. No car. No dinner with the family. If her room hadn't been rented out, she would have been sent there. Adulthood hadn't protected her from, or prepared her for, the wrath of parental punishment, and she still had three days to go.

Profile

Art Colony for One

Todd

When Todd was thrown out of his illegal co-op at the same time as he lost his job, he decided to make the most of his new, abundant free time. He moved back to his parents' house and turned it into his own private artist's colony, working every day on his budding screenplay with the help of a Macintosh Powerbook (which he bought used for half price and is still going strong). He enjoyed all the benefits of a traditional writer's retreat: free rent, free food, all the time in the day to work on his piece, and the equipment to facilitate it. While there were no cocktail events with other artists, Todd used the free phone service to touch base with friends, get feedback on his progress, and discuss the nature of art and writing. A few months and a finished screenplay later, he packed up, moved back to the city, got a job, and started peddling his new artistic wares.

Parents rush in where the NEA fears to tread.

Parents vs. Paris:
A Comparison in Travel

Sample Itinerary of Weekend at Mom and Dad's House

Friday
8:00 P.M. Greyhound arrives. The dynamic duo, Mom and Dad, await with family roadster.

9:00 P.M. Arrival at house. Greet younger brother, dog. Have cocktail with Mom and Dad. Eat dinner favorite that Mom prepared. Stifle a nicotine fit.

11 P.M. Check out your childhood room, which is being renovated. Notice boxes filled with your stuff have been tampered with. Put stuff in guest room. Recognize the irony in being forced to sleep on the sagging guest bed you broke while jumping on it at slumber party. Wish family good night.

12 A.M. Go to cellar to start load of laundry. Have a cigarette. Catch up with dog.

12:30 A.M. Channel surf. Catch up on MTV, Mary Tyler Moore reruns, late movie, late talk shows, infomercials.

2:30 A.M. Bed.

Saturday
7:00 A.M. Dog scratches at door. Wants to go for a walk. Roll over and ignore.

8:00 A.M. Rude awakening. Mom and Dad are golfing. If you don't drive your brother to work now, you won't have the car all day. Say you'd rather be stranded until Mom and Dad return at noon. The dog has a grooming appointment at 10:00 A.M. you must take him to, so you must take the car. Grudgingly drop brother off.

9:00 A.M. Return to house. Take shower. Tape nap.

10:00 A.M. Take dog to groomer. Get Dunkin' Donuts coffee on way home.

11:00 A.M. Eat cereal. Do another load of laundry. Smoke cigarette.

12:00 P.M. Mom and Dad return refreshed. Invite you to lunch. You accept. Pile in car. Mom announces there are a few errands first. Pick up dry cleaning, pick up geraniums, go to neighbor's house to drop off borrowed platter.

1:00 P.M. Swing by historic gardens. Check out the roses. Run into third-grade teacher there. Briefly recap the last fifteen years.

1:30 P.M. Lunch.

4:00 P.M. Check your machine. Return calls. While you're at it, call long-distance friends on your parents' nickel. Chat without looking at the clock.

5:00 P.M. Pick up dog. Make dog wait while you smoke cigarette outside the car.

6:00 P.M. Dinner. Dad grills.

8:00 P.M. Fight with brother over TV. Regret that you won the TV fight when he takes off in the car.

9:00 P.M. Wish Mom and Dad good night.

11:00 P.M. Channel surf.

1:00 A.M. Bed.

Sample Itinerary of a Weekend in Paris

Friday
9:00 P.M. Board airplane, eat dinner, sip wine, stifle nicotine fit, recline seat, sleep.

Saturday
8:00 A.M. Arrive Charles de Gaulle, smoke cigarette, check into cozy Rive Gauche hotel, shower, change.

10:00 A.M. Croissants, cafés au lait, and cigarettes at Les Deux Magots.

11:00 A.M. Visit Musée D'Orsay.

1:00 P.M. Stroll along the Seine. Have lunch and cigarette at Le Petit Plat. Pretend to read *Le Figaro*.

3:00 P.M. Shop for cookware at E. Dehillerin and clothing at Le Samaritaine.

7:00 P.M. Glass of wine at Le Passage. Notice French man taking a seat near you. See him remove his wedding ring. Anticipate watching his rendezvous with mistress. Realize when he strikes up conversation with you that you are the mistress he had in mind. Accept his invitation to dinner at Les Amognes.

9:00 P.M. Enjoy dinner. Realize he will pay the whole bill. Order another bottle of wine. Smoke cigarette. Discover he is over forty years old. When he asks you to hear jazz at Caveau de la Huchette ask him where his wife will be while you are doing so. Hear confession of a troubled separation. Admire photos of the children. Thank him for dinner and leave.

11:00 P.M. Sneak to the *caveau* without him. See striking long-haired bespectacled man without wedding ring sitting alone. Join him. Smoke cigarettes. Drink wine. Laugh with abandon. Kiss the tall French stranger. Give him your business card and tell him to look you up if he is ever in the States. Protest when he says he will never forget you.

2:00 A.M. Return to hotel for sleep.

Sunday
10:00 A.M. Eat brioche and jam. Drink coffee. Smoke cigarettes. Scribble in journal.

12:00 P.M. Visit Père Lachaise cemetery. Greet Gertrude, Alice, Edith, and Jim.

1:00 P.M. Return to Charles de Gaulle, take airplane home.

NO MORE RESTLESS NIGHTS IN ONE-NIGHT CHEAP HOTELS: . . . A REAL VACATION

"ADVENTURE IS THE CHAMPAGNE OF LIFE."

—G. K. CHESTERTON

Every now and then, it's not enough to take a local vacation or visit friends. You've got to go far, far away. When you do, make sure the price is right. If you know what you are doing, it is possible to travel to the ends of the earth without breaking the bank.

The first order of business is to read the box on frequent flying (see Whoring It Up: When to Stray from Your Primary Carrier, page 187). We hope it will change your life, as it has ours. Then consider these other tips for far-flung romps:

- *Make your boss pay.* Try to enjamb the end of a business trip with the beginning of a vacation. If your company flies you somewhere, see if it is at or near anyplace you want to hang out for a few days. If so, take some vacation days and tack them on the end of the business trip. This way, the company picks up half the air bill.

- *Be flexible.* Notice ads in the papers featuring plummeting rates, check regularly with Now Voyager, be willing to get bumped from your flight so that you miss a day of your vacation but win a free round-trip ticket for being a good sport. Having a low-paying job often means having flexibility that power players don't. Use it to your advantage. If you can leave for vacation without too much advance notice, and are not picky about where you go, you will find some great deals.

- *Get a good travel agent.* Would you act as your own attorney in a lawsuit? Would you remove your own appendix? Then why make your own travel plans when there are professionals who do it and *whom you don't have to pay?* That's right, it doesn't cost you a dime to consult people who know the ins and outs of savvy travel. Find a good one, develop a relationship with her, and you'll have a guardian travel angel looking over your shoulder.

- *Vacation in the off-season.* Few people want to go to Barcelona or Paris in March and November. Those who do usually end up paying between three hundred and four hundred dollars for their flights. The hell with summer—things are hot, crowded, touristy, expensive, and in August often closed. If you want to save money, work through the summer and frolic in the fall.

- *Go (with a) native.* You get the most inside experience possible if you travel with a native. Not only will you get to see the nooks and crannies ordinary tourists never do, you'll save money. Your hosts probably have a car they'll shuttle you about in and a house they may want you to stay in, meals they'll want to feed you, interesting neighbors for you to meet. Gone is the fear that you, or your high school French, will be lost.

- *Take a roommate.* Double occupancy is much less expensive than single, and it's usually more fun. When you are with someone else, you can appreciate grandeur and laugh off squalor more easily. A lonely night in a cheap hotel is relentless; with a friend, it's campy.

- *Take a lover.* What's true of apartment rents is true of hotel bills. Try to split it with a lover. If you didn't bring one with you, pick one up when you get there. Don't we all long to say in earnest, "We'll always have Paris?"

- *Travel to hospitable countries.* Certain countries are known for their hospitality to foreigners. Countries that used to be behind the Iron Curtain boast friendly folks who sometimes take travelers in, or at least socialize with them and don't have hang-ups about people who don't speak the language. Hitchhiking remains pretty safe in friendly Ireland, and we have friends who've met Italians on the street and gotten invited in for a glass of wine.

- *Learn something.* Some people feel they are getting the most for their money if they are getting something in return. If you are the sort who never rests and must always keep busy, consider a working vacation. You can learn to cook, build a boat and sail it, excavate, and more. For some, working vacations are a dream come true, for others, they are cheesy opportunities to be trapped with a bunch of strangers and forced to exert themselves. It depends on what you like.

- *Dress up.* Look clean and respectable when you travel, especially if you are flying. This doesn't mean that you need to wear a suit—that's too much; it means you ought to be dressed with enough urban chic to look important and command respect. People who look good are the ones that get upgraded on airplanes, have an easier time with language barriers, get into sacred places that don't allow shorts and T-shirts, and generally have things handed to them because they look like they deserve it.

- *Realize that the more exotic the dirt, the cleaner it appears.* It is strange but true that things you'd never endure at home, you accept gracefully on vacation. Though you may have fancied a chateau as the ideal place to hang your chapeau while in the Pyrenees, if you have no money, you'll settle for a dirty pup tent and probably still find it charming. (It's not just a tent, it's a *French* tent.) The reason may be that if you've paid too much money to be someplace having fun, you'll try to convince yourself, even in the most dire circumstances, that you've succeeded. Or it may be that tolerance in the face of indignity compliments your "when in Rome" notion of yourself as a spontaneous, liberal, rugged adventurer. Whatever the reason, a shack in Madagascar always sounds better than a Hilton in the Ozarks. So travel to the ends of the earth and don't worry that your tight budget won't keep you in style. Your sense of style will conveniently change according to what's affordable.

Profile

They're Going to Graceland

Betsy and Amanda

After Betsy and Amanda were graduated from school, their class-mates took off on cheesy vacations to Fort Lauderdale and Key West. Betsy and Amanda decided if they were going to take a tacky vacation, it would be a kitschy conversation piece as well as a good time. So they booked tickets to Memphis. They were going to Mecca: Graceland.

Betsy has always had a thing for dead celebrities, especially Elvis. Until the Memphis trip, she didn't know much about the man—hadn't seen the movies, knew only a few big songs like "Hound Dog," "Blue Suede Shoes," and "Love Me Tender." But she de-lighted in the empire that is Elvis—the wacky, tacky groupies; the kitschy merchandise; his scandal-mongering relations. His home-town was everything she'd expected and more.

To save money, the two booked tickets for August and stayed in the only cheap hotel they could find during what turned out to be "Elvis Week." The motel, La Quinta, was itself a running joke: the evil, ignorant management; the location (essentially, a Denny's parking lot); the closet that had been converted to a bathroom; the "art," which had been nailed to the walls; the polyester bedspreads; the thieving maid; the stranger vomiting by the window at 3:00 A.M.

They decided to use public transportation to explore the city, rather than rent a car. This meant waiting for buses in ninety-degree heat and enduring the rain that fell when the humidity hit a hundred. Their favorite bus route was, of course, the one that went to the Graceland complex. At Graceland they savored the King's nouveau gauche decorating sense. They saw the Jungle Room (green shag carpeting on ceiling and floor), the *Lisa Marie*, one of Elvis's jets, which sports a queen-size bed and gold-plated seat belt buckles (the *Lisa Marie* boarding passes make great souvenirs); the meditation garden where Elvis is interred; and many other points of interest.

Some nights the two went downtown, where they reveled in the Beale Street blues bars. Other nights they spent at the hotel, quietly ruminating on the King, and, on the night they had to miss the overbooked candlelight vigil, they demolished their motel bathroom by dyeing their hair in it.

Betsy and Amanda still get mileage out of the laughs they had on their pilgrimage to Memphis, proving that if you are brazen, you can turn a silly joke into a great vacation.

Profile

Le Weekend à Paris

Andrea

One morning Andrea noticed an ad in the newspaper posting a round-trip fare to Paris at an exceptionally low four hundred dollars. (Off-season fares have since plummeted to two hundred and fifty dollars, but Andrea ne regret rien.) She told her roommate about the fare, who said, "Let's go." So they did. Naysayers told them that the airfare would be the least of their expenses, but the two forged onward. They took three days off of work, booked the seats, booked a dirt-cheap hotel room over a bar, and visited the French tourist board in New York. There they were able to buy discounted passes for the bus from the airport to the city, three-day bus/metro passes, and three-day museum passes. When they got to Paris, they ate one nice meal. For all the others they ate bread and cheese, which was delicious because it was French bread and French cheese. They hardly spent a dime on anything else.

Four days was plenty of time to see several museums, shops, squares, and sidewalk cafés—and not enough time to waste money on big hotel bills. Andrea believes it was worth every franc.

Profile

Lobbying at the Hilton

Justin

On his way back to New York from Florence, Justin swung by Milan, the design—and Armani—capital of the world. Since he would be there for only one night, he figured that to save money on a hotel, he would just stay up the whole time, take the train back to the airport, arrive there exhausted, and sleep on the plane. He checked his bags at the train station, toured the city, saw the museums and duomo, had dinner, went to a bar, then found a nightclub, where he lounged until it closed unexpectedly early at 2:00 A.M. Entirely spent, he decided he had to find a place to crash for a few hours, so he inquired of a fellow clubber where the best hotels were and was directed to the Hilton. He strode confidently through the Hilton lobby, found the elevators, and took one to a random floor, where he noted how the rooms were numbered. Then he found the mezzanine, where he collapsed into a comfortable armchair. Twenty minutes later he was shaken awake by a hotel official wanting to know what he was doing there. Always elegantly attired, well spoken, and polite, Justin explained that his parents were staying in the hotel and that he would get in trouble for waking them by coming in so late. The official asked him which room his parents were in. Justin didn't miss a beat when he told him one of the numbers he'd noticed upstairs. When the hotel official asked Justin to follow him, Justin figured he was being shown the door. He wasn't. He was being shown the downstairs bar/lounge, whose big, green leather banquettes, the manager assured him, would be more comfortable than a chair. Justin awakened to a "buon giorno" from the concierge, who took the trouble to walk him to the nearby train station where Justin showered in a day hotel before boarding his plane. Justin has fond memories of sweet dreams in Milan.

FULL HOUSE: SUMMER SHARES

Another real vacation idea involves real estate: the summer share. It feels very grown up to occupy a summer house—like a dry run for actual ownership—but with adulthood comes adult responsibilities: Renting a house for the summer takes organization. Someone has to find the right house, negotiate the subletting terms, round up a bunch of people who want to join the share, arrange payment, and then take care of the house.

Summer shares are not for everyone: They can be very expensive (prices vary wildly depending on where in the country you live, what kind of house you rent, and how many people are involved). They demand commitment; as with a gym membership, if you've already paid for it, you'll feel guilty if you don't use it enough. They demand compromise; you have to be flexible if you are going to share a space with eight or ten other people. (Rainy days in a crowded house especially test the limits of one's tolerance.)

If you like taking on big long-term projects, try a share. But first consider the following tips:

Organize It Yourself

If you do all the research of finding a house and finding bodies to fill it you will be at an economic and entertainment advantage. You can select people you know and like—and who you know can pay the rent (up front, usually)—and you can divvy up the costs so that you don't pay anything. This is not slimy or unusual. The person who organizes has to get everything in order and bears the burden of signing the lease and taking responsibility for the place. If you are willing to bite off all that, you shouldn't have to chew on rent as well.

Know What You Are Getting Into

If you are simply joining a share, you should find one through friends or friends of friends. We do not recommend you cast your lot with people whose habits and sensibilities are wild cards. Also know what the deal is. What exactly does your money buy? Do you get your own bed? How is the choice of rooms determined? Does everyone pay the same amount? Do you get every weekend or every other?

Of course, in order to really FYI, it's best to find summer homes to crash at, rather than committing to one yourself. You'll enjoy a variety of people and locations and you won't have to pay for much more than a gift.

Profile

THE LILY BART OF THE NINETIES

MEAGHAN

Like Edith Wharton's heroine in *The House of Mirth*, Meaghan is a cultured freeloader. Summer is peak season for Meaghan. She has one goal and she is determined to stick to it: to escape the city every weekend from Memorial Day through Labor Day without paying rent for a share. She could just drop in on her parents each weekend, vegetate on their couch, channel surf, and eat, but where would the fun lie? Meaghan aims higher: She uses her parents' home near the lake as a down payment for country home crashing.

Before summer begins, she hosts a cocktail party at her parents' home, charming prospective hosts with her family's liquor cabinet and bulging refrigerator. As summer Wednesdays approach, Meaghan's itchy dialing finger gets to work making calls to friends with country homes (and those whose parents have them too). After hellos and how are yous have been exchanged, she cuts to the chase. She asks her friends what they are doing for the weekend. They tell her and then they ask what she is doing and invite her to join them. She tells them she is weighing two other invitations. They invariably tell her she should go with them instead. Meaghan says she'll think about it and call them back the next day.

On Thursday, Meaghan calls the friend to say that she'd be delighted to join them for the weekend. She intimates that their offer sounds much more fun than the two decoys. Then she makes them glad to have her. She will be an indispensible addition to their weekend fun: She is in the mood to barbecue, mix refreshing margaritas and martinis, and offer her parents' car for the whole weekend.

When she arrives she does so with a housewarming gift, usually a nice tin of cookies or some tea. And, depending on the gender of the host, she may even send a thank you gift—for women and parents, flowers and a note, for male peers, a gift is usually unnecessary. Her considerate and generous manner always gives way to more invites, and more invites give way to a summer well spent, away from the humid city.

ESCAPE: GO WHEN THE GOING IS GOOD

If visiting the ends of the earth or practically owning real estate with a summer share doesn't accommodate your leisure needs, it's time to quit your job and run away. Unless you are a vice president or own stock in your firm, you have little to lose by pulling up stakes and taking off. There is probably no damage done, and if there is, you are young and spry enough to bounce back with no trouble.

Live Light

Because they care about the junk they've collected, pack rats can't flee their homes easily. Pack rats break a sweat at the thought of having to throw away any of their stuff and live in another country without a steady paycheck and health insurance. Free spirits usually live in furnished sublets; the thought of owning a piece of furniture gives them a rash. If you are one of the unhappy few in whom the qualities of both pack rat and free spirit dwell, you had better hope Mom and Dad haven't refinished the attic yet.

Embrace Job Fate

It's much easier to leave a job you dislike or feel is going nowhere than one with promise. It's also easier to leave town when your company is unstable or folds. Unpleasantness in the workplace enables you to convince yourself that you are not fickle—your worsening workplace is a sign from God that you should take some time to regroup on a commune in the Czech Republic. Believing in divine intervention eases guilt and makes explaining things to your family simpler.

Leave While You Still Have Time

There is a program that enables people who were graduated from college no more than a year prior, to work legally in certain countries, like Great Britain. If you leave within six months of your college graduation, you have a chance of getting a legitimate job. If you do it after that, you will have to work under the table.

Enroll in a Life Deferral Plan

If you really hate working and want to get away, apply to graduate school. Go to one in a foreign country and it will feel more like a vacation. We understand that a year in an American graduate program seems longer than three in a Turkish prison.

Profile

PERMANENT VACATION

David

David was never much for office work, but at his mother's nagging he took a low-paying job that involved answering phones and pushing paper for forty plus hours a week. He enjoyed life after hours going out with friends, painting, and playing in his band. A man of few material needs, David found he was actually able to squirrel away some money.

The day his boss quit, the sky opened up for David. This was a sign from the heavens that he should quit too. So he did. He packed his bags, parceled out his few belongings among his mother and his friends, and departed for Mexico with the few pesos he'd saved. He stayed there for several months, perfecting his Spanish, eating beans, and having a grand old time. When he returned, he called up friends at his old job and discovered that they were desperately under-staffed. They took David on as a freelancer. Now he makes more money per hour, doing more interesting work than he did when he was on the payroll.

Some vacations pay off in spades.

A FEW WORDS ON FREQUENT FLYING

"SOME PEOPLE WILL SELL THEIR SOULS FOR A FREE RIDE ON AN AIR-PLANE."

—JACQUELINE BOUVIER KENNEDY ONASSIS

If far-flung travel is a priority for you, then so should organizing your frequent flyer programs. Justin Powell, *very* frequent flyer, has traveled all over Europe mostly on free miles, which he cultivates diligently. Some people (not any we know, mind you) have stock portfolios; Justin has a miles portfolio. This section reflects his expert advice on how to maintain your miles.

Justin's Advice

SIGN UP FOR EVERY MAJOR FREQUENT FLYER MILES PROGRAM *NOW.* Don't wait until you go somewhere; there's probably a bonus for signing up or a first-flight bonus awarded after membership. Signing up right away ensures you will start receiving information soon, which will aid your travel research. Put all of the airlines' phone numbers in your Filofax beside your personal frequent traveler numbers.

GET ORGANIZED. Buy a three-ring binder with plastic sleeves on the covers. File all the mail you receive from the airlines in the binder according to airline. Place time-sensitive schedule and bonus information in the sleeves for easy access. Read every piece of mail you receive from the airlines (especially the back page of their flyers, which lists seasonal bonus information). Don't discard frequent flyer reading material until long after it has expired. Some promotions are easily extended, so if you think you've missed a deadline, speak up and try to get the benefits anyway.

ANALYZE YOUR TRAVEL PATTERNS TO MAXIMIZE YOUR MILEAGE. Are there places you must fly every year? Your parents' home for Thanksgiving and Christmas? An annual conference for work? Choose a principal airline to cultivate based on its superior service to your intended destination. For example, Justin's family lives in Charlottesville, which has a small airport serviced best by USAir. Since he must go there at least three times a year, guaranteeing him frequent flyer points, Justin tries to make every mile he earns go to his USAir account.

COMPARE BEFORE YOU BUY A TICKET ANYWHERE. Check the prices at unprofitable airlines. Because they desperately need to increase volume quickly, they usually offer deals. Their service isn't usually any worse than that of the other airlines, so it's worth a shot. (Some people cut corners by going with small, fly-by-night airlines; we favor the better-established companies.)

Call the reservations and frequent flyer desks of airlines at unusual times. At off hours the people manning the lines will have some time. Chat them up about deals. They almost always have inside information they are willing to divulge if they aren't busy and you are friendly and curious. You may even try to beg for bargains, which we have found to work occasionally (and may save the airline from paying the ten-to-fifteen-percent travel agent's commission).

Collect every complimentary inflight magazine of every flight you take. There are sometimes special deals hidden within them: credit card deals, flight specials, etc.

Heed newspaper ads (usually located in the first section of the paper). These ads are often the first sign of deals. Extrapolate as you read. If there is a great fare to Frankfurt, chances are there is a competitive one to Amsterdam (and even cheaper ones to London and Paris). And it's likely that every airline will be offering competing fares, so you'll have your pick of carrier.

DO THE MATH. Realize that the most economically advantageous route between two airports is never a straight line, so, if you can avoid it, don't fly nonstop; fly via a hub, preferably one that breaks the distance up unequally. For instance, on a flight from Los Angeles to New York, go via Atlanta rather than St. Louis. The reason: The distance between Los Angeles and Atlanta is many miles more than the distance between Los Angeles and St. Louis. Likewise, the distance between Atlanta and New York is many miles more than the distance between St. Louis and New York. Hence, the sum of miles from Los Angeles to New York via St. Louis is the same as if you'd never stopped, whereas it is much greater if you add Atlanta to the equation. You will earn many more miles if you don't fly along the hypotenuse. (Speaking of St. Louis, because its hub is there and it has no major partner airline, TWA is probably not your best choice of a principal airline.)

This may seem like a sacrifice of time, but when you can't afford to waste money (be it in the form of cash or mileage points), wasting time becomes a necessity. Bring a book and a Walkman, and make the best of it. If you pay attention to the connection times, and are savvy at planning, sometimes it may not take much more time to go out of your way for a few miles. For example, it takes nearly the same amount of time—door to door—to go from New York to Berlin via Boston as it does to go nonstop. Why? A nonstop international flight would likely leave from JFK, which is the airport located farthest away from New York City. It is the largest airport, the one most difficult to travel within. The plane would likely be very large, taking a long time to board. A flight to Boston, on the other hand, would depart from LaGuardia, a smaller airport located closer to Manhattan. On a domestic flight, the aircraft would be smaller, easier to board, and would not require an arrival two hours before departure. Boston's Logan is a smaller airport, where connection hassles are minimized. The flight through Boston adds many more miles than it does hours to your total travel time, and may even save some money (the cost of a cab to JFK vs. LaGuardia, for instance) as well as hassles.

TRY TO REACH AN "ELITE" STATUS. Your goal is to travel as a gold card member, which means that you must earn something like thirty thousand miles a year (plans vary) without bonus miles.

Once you become an elite member of your frequent flyer program, your airline will go out of its way to keep you, and will offer nice perks. Elite members board flights first with business and first-class travelers. They get to hang out in the private lounge before the flight leaves, sipping complimentary beverages. They have access to a private reservations phone number. Their baggage is given priority handling. Most significantly, elite members earn an extra twenty-five percent bonus for every mile they earn.

In addition to racking up miles any which way you can, to become elite you must act wealthier and more important than you are. When the airline sends surveys, always complete them with enthusiastic lies, and return them promptly (this alone may earn you miles). Tell the airline you make a hundred thousand dollars a year, travel all the time in business class, and are faithful to no one carrier. This will make them court you. The mailings will become more personal, hungrier, and the deals will be easier to understand.

MAKE IT WORTH THE TRIP. When you spend your hard-earned miles, make sure you aren't selling yourself short. A free trip in the contiguous forty-eight states is rarely worth it. A trip from Honolulu to Washington, D.C., is. A trip from Dallas to Anchorage is. A trip to Europe or Asia is.

Never spend frequent flyer miles on something as frivolous as a class upgrade, unless that's all you can be bothered to spend them on.

Earning Miles

CREDIT CARDS. The only time you should ever consider paying a credit card fee is on a card that earns frequent flyer miles with every purchase. It is a bitter pill, as the annual fees are high (usually about fifty-five dollars) and they are rarely negotiable. If you decide to dedicate yourself to the frequent flyer way, however, a frequent flyer credit card is imperative. It is the easiest way to earn miles: For every dollar you put on the card you earn a mile. If you have a mile-earning card, put everything on it. Everything: groceries, books, clothing, graduate school tuition. *Everything*, or it's not worth it. (Cash advances, taboo in all but dire circumstances, and balance transfers don't earn frequent flyer points.)

Ideally you should get a corporate American Express card from your company and link it to a frequent flyer miles account of your own. That way every free business lunch is a free mile. Be careful about putting personal things on it: Remember, AmEx must be paid in full at the end of every month.

Whoring It Up: When to Stray From Your Primary Carrier

Admit it: When you are not absolutely satisfied, your eye wanders. Faithfulness is good, but sometimes it pays to play around. When another airline makes you an offer you can refuse, don't. Avoid foolish consistencies in the air as on the ground. Waywardness is applauded in the following cases:

Outrageous Fares
Some fares can't be beat and are worth snapping up even if they are a wash milewise. This happens at off-peak times of the year. All of Europe is on sale in February and March, and sometimes October and November. The American South is usually on sale in July and August, when no one wants to go there.

Bonus Miles

If the fares are all the same, but someone is offering triple mileage, go with that carrier. It won't be hard to make up the difference for a freebie after a mileage bonanza.

Packages

City-hopping deals like Lufthansa's Discover Europe deal, in which you can visit several cities for the price of one, are well worth it.

Youth Deals

Under twenty-six years old? How nice for you. You get deals all over the place, ranging from shuttles to intercontinental flights. Make sure you tell your airline or travel agent your age as you research deals. (This is one of few times when you want to act as young as you are.)

Profile

Minibar Macadamia Nuts

ANNE

For a week last year, guests to Anne's modest apartment were offered macadamia nuts. Her friends scratched their heads. Was it a strange personality quirk that Anne favored expensive nuts as a snack over something more economical like Cheerios? Was she living beyond her means and recklessly charging exotic sundries at the grocery store? Was she making more money at her publicist's job than she was letting on?

When people remarked on the inconsistency in Anne's lifestyle, she clarified. Despite her underling status, her company had sent her on a business trip. Her hotel room came equipped with a minibar chock full o' nuts and other delights, which Anne transferred to her luggage before she checked out.

Always thinking of others, Anne brought the treasures home and treated her friends and roommates. They feasted on the delights of the business class until the stash was exhausted. Follow Anne's lead: If the nuts are on the company, make sure they are on your person as you leave the hotel.

Profile

SOMETHING FOR NOTHING

Paul

Paul quit his crummy job and bought a one-way ticket to Greece for a much-needed, albeit unaffordable, vacation. He frolicked in the sun, island hopped, and generally unwound. Perhaps he unwound just a bit too much, because with no money and little credit left, he suddenly found that he could not live without a certain Versace jacket calling his name in a small shop in Athens. With his credit completely exhausted but his appreciation of rustic leisure intact, he made two phone calls. One to his travel agent uncle, whom he convinced to wire him a return ticket to New York City; the other to his friends, who agreed to pick him up, victorious, at JFK.

Paul had all he needed to survive the few days it would take to get home (Mykonos to Athens, Athens to Brussels, Brussels to New York) except food. What did he do? From Mykonos to Athens, he suffered. At the Athens airport he slept upright in a plastic chair and charmed knapsack cookies from the American college girls he met. In Brussels, his tolerance of frugality broke. He was dirty and unshaven. He couldn't face his friends like that.

At the Brussels airport Paul collected his thoughts. He realized that he'd never be able to talk his way into the local fifteen-dollar-a-night hostel. Those places have seen impoverished privilege before and are unsympathetic. He was more likely to be able to finesse his way into the Ritz. Donning his new designer jacket, and putting his chin up, he used the courtesy phones to call a car to take him to the hotel. There he offered his spent Visa card and was shown to his room. He showered, shaved, changed his clothes, repacked his suit-cases, and waited for the management to arrive to throw him out. They never came. He went to sleep, awoke the next morning, checked out, had a car take him to his flight, and arrived at JFK looking spiffy and very well rested.

Moral: Clothing and demeanor speak louder than money. Dare to do it.

Profile

Aisha at the Airport

Unwilling to endure the endless flight back from Pakistan to the United States in the coach section, Aisha spent the money on a first-class ticket. When she arrived at the airport to check in, however, she was informed that her seat had been given away and that she could go only via coach. Very upset, Aisha firmly insisted upon being given her rightful seat. The authorities did not respond. She turned up the volume, loudly demanding her seat. Again, no response. Finally, she turned on the waterworks and cried. Between each hysterical sob, she told them about her history of back trouble, that she couldn't sit for long periods of time without experiencing excruciating pain. A crowd gathered. Managers were called to the scene. They reiterated that the only seat available was in coach. Grudgingly, Aisha took the seat. As soon as the airplane was prepared for takeoff, a stewardess asked Aisha to please follow her. Aisha did—through coach and business class, up the staircase through first class, and finally through a door near the cockpit that led to a small room with a narrow bed in it. Aisha spent the long flight home reclined in the captain's cozy private quarters.